On the Bell Lap, Walking Among Giants

Becoming a Sorcerer's Apprentice

1961 - 1973

By: Herbert A. (Tag) Waggener

Books by the Author

Released, perhaps in further revision:

Herb, My Early Story
First A Panther, Now A Bulldog
The Education and Domestication of a Bulldog
On the Bell Lap, Walking Among Giants
Teletype, We Made That Data Move!

These books are available from http://www.lulu.com, http://www.amazon.com, and the author at: 7282 178th Street, Chippewa Falls WI 54729.

In Progress:

Electron Beams, Water Jets, and Medical Devices
From Employment to Independent

Left half of Murray Hill NJ Bell Labs Complex in 2009.
My office was on the second floor of Building 2, foreground.
The "Elephant House" is located just behind building 2.
Center building (R) was added in late 70's or early 80's.

(Downloaded from Google Earth, 2010)

Right Half of Murray Hill Bell Labs Complex in 2009
The Research Division occupied most of Building 1,
in foreground. In 1961, I checked in with relocation staff
located in Building 3, indicated by hand image.
Arnold Auditorium is at far right.
Center Building (L) was added in late 70's or early 80's.
My process facility was located in 1E358 in 1970.

(Downloaded from Google Earth, 2010)

On The Bell Lap, Walking Among *Giants*

Becoming a Sorcerer's Apprentice

1961-1973

By Herbert A. Waggener

(Aka Tag, Herb, or Herbie)

16 June 2010

© 2010 Herbert A. Waggener

All rights reserved. No part of this book may be used or reproduced in any manner whatsoever without written permission by the author.

ISBN 978-0-557-35243-2

Table of Contents

Table of Contents xi
  Acknowledgement 15
  Preface 17

Chapter 1 – On to MURRAY HILL 21
  Wending Our Way to and Through New Jersey, Late July 1961 21
  My Earliest Experiences With the Personnel Department at BTL 31
  47 Dogwood Lane, a Really Nice Place For Kids 34
  Study, Study, Study, and Maybe a Little Work 36
  Taco, or - Four More Feet Join our Family 40
  A Little Work 43

Chapter 2 - My First Work Assignment 1961-1963 45
  Find the Balls of Solder! 45
  A Happy Coincidence - Infrared Alignment 46
  A Fatal Error in Procedure, not Easily Overcome 48
  Telstar - The First Communication Satellite - 1962 50
  The Nike Surface to Air Missile Systems and Case Charges 54
  A Christmas Party I Didn't Attend 56
  My First (Almost) Merit Review - 1962 58
  Some things To Do, Or Not 61
  YMCA Indian Guides, and a Delaware River Canoe Trip 63
  Vacations are to be Scheduled in July 65
  CDT Is Completed, But Am I Finished? - June 1963 ... 66
  I Attend my First IEEE International Device Meeting .. 68

First Rotation - My Niobium Tin (non) Superconductors 75
Second Rotation - Thin Film Technology - 1963 77
ECS, Pittsburgh PA – My First Talk - 1963 80
100 Walton Avenue, Smaller and Cheaper 85
I Build a Superb FM Stereo Receiver After Hours 89
My Second (or Third) IEEE IEDM 94

Chapter 3 - Semiconductors 97
Some Integrated Circuit Problems Needing Solution for AT&T Systems 97
Performance Limitations of Early Bipolar Integrated Circuits 98
Reliability and Cost, Reliability and Cost 100
Martin Lepselter Conceives Beam Leads 101
Third Rotation - Integrated Circuits Again - 1964 104
Early AIM Technology Development, Murray Hill 108
Beam Leads Go Public at the IEDM – Dec 1964 115
Sand Blasting and Light Activated Etching (cough, sneeze, or run away) 116
A First Try at Anisotropic Etching 119
End-Marked AIM pnpn arrays with Air Crossovers and Fuses 125
The Alkali Metal Hydroxide / Alcohol Etchants - 1966 126
We Buy a House Foundation in NJ (Apr 66) and are Transferred to Allentown Pennsylvania (Jul 66) 128

Chapter 4 – The Allentown Experience - July 1966 135
Ready, Set, Process AIM Devices 139
We Buy a House in Allentown – 1967 142
We Go to Press, and Publicly Disclose the AIM Technology 146
Sam Broydo Analyzes Photo Transistor Arrays –1968 148
My Final Year Working at Allentown –1968 151
Electroplating Control for Beam Leads – Another Masterpiece - 1968 153

Some Events Leading to a Very, Very Foolish Action . 155
My Most Foolish Action, Bad Boss Bashing – mid 1967 or early 1968 161

Chapter 5 – My Return to Murray Hill and Redemption – 1969 165

The 1969 ISSCC Best Paper Award 169
Commuting and Working on the Non-Verbal Side of My Brain 172
A Black 1964 Corvair, My Supercoupe - 1969 173
My Next Big Achievement - Electrochemically Controlled Thinning - 1969 174
Al MacRae Becomes my Mentor and Champion – Late 1969 181
Enter John Dalton and Room 1E358 – Mid 1970 187
Sigurd Waaben and His Two-Diode Memory - 1970 ... 189
Silicon on Insulator 193
More Electrochemistry - That Silicon Has Potential! – Late 1970 194
My Promotion to Supervisor - December 1970 197
Sam Broydo – Physicist, Superb Analyst, and Friend – Early 1971 199
Pete Panousis and a Fortuitous Hallway Technical Meeting Early 1971 201
Mom and Dad Return to Appleton City, 1971 205

Chapter 6 - New Directions for Semiconductor Development 209

Phase 1 and Phase 2 are Defined – May 1971 209
The Phase 2 Structure is Revealed - May 1971 213
I Upgrade to a Canary Yellow 1965 Corvair 217
I Am "Invited" to the Hot-Seat Meeting, a New Platform 218
Process Setup Continues 219
Training for New Bell Labs Supervisors 222
How Do We Effectively Communicate Upwards? 226

I Discover and Capture a Stray ISI Scanning Electron Microscope 229
The Cat Pee Syndrome is Named............................... 231
Memory Chip Masks Available, My Activities Split 233
Next target, World's Largest CCD Devices 234
A Super Wafer is Fabricated! OOPS! Superwafer Dies!! 237
1E358 ->->->->-> "Crash Pad" 239
Sam Broydo and I Continue to Analyze Phase 2 Devices. 245
We Take Command of the BPL – Both Shifts! 247
The Brushes are a Problem – We Use Water Spray 249
High Pressure Pure Water Spray = Static Generator. 251
The Lithography Solution – Improve Control and Minimize Changes 252
Massive Aluminum Oven Walls and Simplified Control Practices 253
Superwafer Wounds are Healed, With Little Scarring 255
We Study Putting Beam Leads on Aluminum 257
More Corvair Tales 258

Chapter 7 – Phase 2 Declared a Success
.... 265
Two Samari Present Talks at ECS, Miami FL............. 265
Samari Warriors 267
A Management Change – Phil Boddy Takes Over – April 1973 270
The Stinking Ship – Imus Brightens my Mornings........ 274
The Teletype Visit, Then Intel - 1973 279
Teletype It Is! 287
The Transfer Process Begins!...................................... 293
Postscript 295
Appendix 1 – HAW Patents Held or Co-held as of June 2010 300

Acknowledgement

I thank Fred L. Alexander, originally from Rockville and Appleton City Missouri, for pointing recruiters in my direction, and thereby giving me the opportunity to work at Bell Labs.

I thank Martin P. Lepselter and Alfred U. MacRae for their influence on my career and their help in reconstituting some early recollections. Marty's work gave me something of substance to work on, and his timely summons resulted in my return to Murray Hill from Allentown, correcting a career trajectory otherwise headed towards oblivion. As my Department Head, Al insisted that I properly document my work, put me on track to obtaining recognition, promoted me to Supervisor, and supplied a lot of helpful recalibration. To both of these men, I am profoundly grateful.

I thank Sam Broydo who has likewise had an enormous influence on my thinking processes. His intellect and friendship have had a positive impact on my later career. I consider the time working with Sam some of the more productive in my life. His insight and skills are much appreciated. Sam also took most of the photographs of BTL people shown in this book. The photos were taken just before or at my going away party.

I cannot emphasize enough the positive effect of working with the caliber of individuals that inhabited Bell Telephone Labs in that era. From Nobel Prize winners to technicians, the intellectual ability was very, very high, and some of it rubbed off onto the group at large. It was sometimes hard to tell the great from the rest of us mortals, but the personal effect on me was almost magical.

I have found that I learned from all of my immediate superiors, however hard the experience was for them, so they each bear some responsibility for the end result. They know who they are.

Our thinking processes are composites of all those people with whom we have interacted in our earlier lives, and I have had many mentors having both large and small impact. In chronological order, some of these were:

Father Wilson E. Waggener Sr. bought me my first science book, and demanded a lot of me.
Mother Mary Waggener pushed and believed in me.
Aunt Leota Elwell gave me chemistry sets, glassware, and other science gifts, and encouragement.
Uncle Atkin Whitten nurtured my sense of humor.
Uncle Knute Knutson provided me with inspiration.
Ernie Goode taught me metal machining.
Earle Morgan taught me some aeronautics, logarithms, and use of the slide rule.
Teacher John Miles taught me math, chemistry, integrity, and perseverance.
Wilson E. Waggener Jr. showed me what could be accomplished.
Principal Ola Kavanaugh taught me English.
Coach Ray Ballock taught me the value of teamwork and organization.
Dr. Nelson M. Duller gave me a job, guidance, and support at M. U.
Julia Abbot gave me support, a job, and an office in the Chemistry Building at M. U.
Ed Scott gave me friendship and support at M. U., in San Diego, and later on in life.
W. H. Craft and John Sullivan assisted me while I was at Bell Labs, Murray Hill, New Jersey.

Preface

I was born in 1936, a towheaded blond kid who liked to smile a lot and get in my share of trouble, just like millions of other kids around the world. Due to a number of circumstances, my family moved around a lot, so each year I faced a new group of classmates, most of whom knew each other from previous years. In grade school, this made life tough for me, and the fact that I was fairly smart made things worse. Nonetheless, I found ways to cope. I was not athletically gifted, but was tough enough to neutralize the bullies, and make a fair showing at sports. This helped a lot, and I found that I would soon fit in fairly well, with only a few new dents and bruises. Somewhere around fourth or fifth grade, I discovered science, and from that time on I was fixed on learning more and more about the workings of the world around me.

When I entered high school in Missouri, I lived in one place for all four years, so other than my first year, fitting in was less of a problem. I again did not excel in sports, but played basketball and football well enough to earn a letter or two. I continued to love the sciences, but also discovered girls and cars. Now I had not one but four areas of great interest, science, sports, girls, cars, and in the summers, worked full time at my Dad's sawmill. I was fortunate to find several mentors who helped me to keep on a forward path. I was smart, but I was not at the head of my class when I graduated. I just could not bring myself to concentrate hard enough to stand at the top. I enrolled in the University of Missouri at Columbia, with a major in Physics. Upon enrollment, I became a Missouri University Tiger!

At MU, I soon exhibited some talent for physics and math, even though I was taking a full course load and working full time throughout these four years. In the second year, I was achieving excellence in my physics courses, and was awarded the first of several scholarships, and loaded up on physics and math courses. In the second half of my third year, I joined a fraternity to round out my education. I was elected President of the local Physics Club. By the end of my third year, I had finished almost enough courses to graduate. In my fourth year, I became President of the Fraternity, dated several women, became engaged to be married, and academically crashed and burned! I decided to get a masters Degree in Physics at San Diego State College (SDSC). In August, Judith Kerrigan and I were married in Des Moines Iowa, and we soon traveled to California where I would become an SDSC Aztec. When we arrived in San Diego California, we initially moved into a studio apartment located on El Cajon Boulevard, about a mile or so from SDSC, because San Diego State could only offer me a half-time teaching position.

While we lived in our temporary hovel, brother Buddy's second child, Wade Evan Waggener was born in Kansas City Missouri. I would not have an opportunity to see the new addition to our extended family for some time.

At SDSC, I again began to excel academically, and during the second semester, our economic outlook also improved, because I was able to get more teaching time. We took advantage of our improved income and moved into better quarters, a little closer to school. Our first son, Mark, was born in June of 1959. I joined The Navy Electronics Lab, NEL, on Point Loma, and would complete my Master of Science Degree at night. We moved into a superior apartment in Mission Beach where the onshore breezes kept us perhaps 20 degrees or so cooler. Mission Beach was a lot further away from school but not far from work at NEL.

We thoroughly enjoyed the Southern California amenities: Lots of sunshine, semi translucent air, azure skies, sparkling white sand beaches, and some great surfing. Best of all, but a little scary, was the birth of our two twins, John (boy) and Shawn (girl). Our twins were born a little prematurely, but soon began to put on weight, and were healthy happy kids.

While I worked at NEL, I was schooled in underwater acoustics, and participated in several voyages on the research submarine USS Baya. I learned a lot, and the work was interesting as well as important, but when I received an offer from the then-famous Bell Telephone Laboratories at Murray Hill New Jersey, I jumped at the chance.

This book contains some of my memories of life while at Bell Labs, the first time around.

Chapter 1 – On to MURRAY HILL

Wending Our Way to and Through New Jersey, Late July 1961

I had been unhappy with my inability to test my merit at the Navy Electronics Lab at San Diego, and had been offered a job at the world's then-most prestigious research and development organization, Bell Telephone Laboratory. What was even better, I would be working at their headquarters in Murray Hill New Jersey, with the cream of the cream. I was to be attached to the components division, and would be working on silicon device technology. I had no idea in what way that I would be useful, since my sole practical background in semiconductors consisted of making simple circuits with commercial transistors such as the Sylvania CK722, and GE 2N123 devices then readily available commercially.

Following my interview at various Bell Labs locations, I had indicated a preference for the Massachusetts facility at

North Andover, because my training at the Navy Electronics Lab had provided me with an excellent foundation with the mathematical physics of transducers and I had some familiarity with underwater sound. Thus, when I was offered a position working on semiconductors in Murray Hill, I had mixed emotions. On the one hand, I would be rubbing elbows with the best of the best in the world of industrial research and development. On the other hand, I would be operating in a new field for which I had little preparation. During my earlier schooling, I had sometimes excelled, often performed acceptably, and I had also experienced disaster, equivalent to crashing and burning. I had long been aware of my limitations, and success in the future was not assured. Nonetheless, my internal qualms were rapidly overcome, and I eagerly looked forward to the challenge of working at Bell Labs. On our last night in San Diego, we stayed in friend Ed Scott's apartment in San Diego. Ed Scott, a fellow graduate of the University of Missouri, had let us sleep in his apartment because he was momentarily at point Mugu working on a prototype communication system. Other friends, Karen and John Christian, loaned us their credit card to make sure that we could make it to the East coast in case of emergency. With the support of Ed Scott, John and Karen Christian, my stalwart crew of Judy, Mark, John, and Shawn set out for New Jersey, around two thousand miles away, driving our well-worn 1954 Chevy two-tone green sedan.

We left San Diego late in the evening, taking the southern route to get across the Mohave Desert at night. The trip through the mountains east of San Diego was crisp and cool, but, as we descended to the desert floor, the temperature rose to the high 90's. At first, the humidity was very low, and sweat evaporated upon contact with the breeze from the open car windows. This dry baking condition soon ended as we reached the vicinity of the All American Canal, where the relative humidity also rose to the high 90's, and the car became a sauna, only we were not wearing Turkish towels. In addition, the air also became filled with very large juicy insects.

The insects were both numerous and gelatinous. When they hit the windshield, they quickly formed a translucent blob of goo that the windshield wipers could only spread into large streaked regions. The bug hits were so numerous that we were quickly forced to stop and physically remove the layer of translucent gunk from the windshield with one of the many spare diapers we had with us. We could then proceed for a while until the cleaning had to be repeated again. Thank goodness, we had an ample supply of diapers, most of which were unused. At the end of the first night, we stayed in a small motel in Gila Bend, New Mexico. The motel had a swimming pool, but the water was too hot to make swimming attractive. We took a shower instead. It was not possible to tell the difference between the hot and cold-water taps, but at least we could remove the road dirt from our bodies and I could get most if not all of the bug juice from my hands and from under my fingernails. Leaving Gila Bend next morning, we soon turned north to pick up Route 66, climbing up into the high plateau country of New Mexico, and found the going much more hospitable. The temperature was still fairly high, but the arid air was truly welcome.

We reached Buckeye, turned east to Phoenix, and soon reached Flagstaff one hundred sixty miles or so further north. The six thousand foot elevation of the Colorado Plateau meant much lower temperatures and humidity. Relief at last! We had been worried about keeping the kids hydrated, so with the more favorable conditions, this concern soon faded away. We had that situation under control. Somewhere between Flagstaff and Oklahoma City, John and Shawn began holding onto the back of the front seat, standing up to better see their surroundings. We were ecstatic! It was a good omen indeed!

When we reached Oklahoma City, we turned north toward Kansas City where Mom and Dad were staying in an apartment. Dad had apparently burned out on selling, and was working as a carpenter building silos for intercontinental missiles, and working on the Interstate System being built in the area. According to Suzanne, Mom either had been or was working as a waitress to occupy her time and add to the family coffers. Suzanne was also living in KC at the time but was living in another separate apartment. Suzanne was working as an executive secretary for the President of Hallmark Corporation at their headquarters in Kansas City.

We stayed with Mom and Dad Waggener for a few days and while in Kansas City met Suzanne's fiancé, Mr. Tom Mower, a tall, good-looking guy with novel and interesting mannerisms. He was at once serious and hilarious. Tom was a graduate of Kansas University, where he had played varsity football. When we met him, he was a successful drug salesman for Winthrop Labs. I recall that we had dinner with Suz and Tom at a local hangout featuring peanut shells littering the floor. Tom had an engaging manner with exaggerated body motions and many fascinating stories, delivered in humorous ways. He retained his unique storytelling technique until his death in 2007.

While we were staying with Mom and Dad in Kansas City, we were all invited to dinner with John Robert and Mary Alice Waggener. This John Waggener was the son of great uncle Jeptha, and so was a cousin of Dad. We enjoyed the time together, and ate a great meal. Mark especially enjoyed the green beans, fresh from the garden. He would first smash them with his utensils or clenched fist and then devour them, calling "More! More!" until all green paste and remnants were gone. Suzanne remembers that at some point, hyper-mobile John and Shawn were placed in an improvised playpen, a large plastic laundry basket, with a few toys, where they played happily. The kids were the center of attention, and Judy and I were proud of them and their behavior.

We left Kansas City to join the Kerrigans in Des Moines, where Judy's pals inundated the Kerrigan house to see their old friend and her children. Jack and Mary Jane likewise invited their friends over to proudly display their descendents. We could only stay a few days, because the starting time at Bell labs had been prearranged to meet a training schedule.

We left Mark, John, and Shawn with the Kerrigans in Des Moines according to our prior plan. When we arrived in New Jersey, we had to find a place to stay, report for work, find a place to live, and install our family. The route from Des Moines took us south of Chicago, along Interstates through Indiana and Ohio, the Pennsylvania Turnpike, and finally along US Highway 22 from Harrisburg, Pennsylvania to the vicinity of Plainfield, New Jersey, just southwest of Newark.

The portion of US 22 in Eastern New Jersey consisted almost entirely of strip malls and individual businesses which had arisen over many decades, so the region was really, really ugly and unappealing. We found an inexpensive motel located on the outskirts of the extended strip mall area located in South Plainfield. The climate in New Jersey in July is hot and very humid, not as hot as Gila Bend, but pretty awful. Fortunately, our tiny room had a window air conditioner. We were to stay at the motel as I went to work until we found more suitable quarters. I am not sure, but I think that the Labs paid for temporary housing, but in any case, we continued to pinch pennies by staying in the little motel until we found a permanent place to live. Pinching pennies had become a way of life, a problem that still haunts me to this day. I think that my right thumb and forefinger have developed a permanent but definite copper tint, and indentations corresponding to clenching coins.

Just north and west of the motel, the dreary appearance of the Route 22 strip gives way to low rolling hills (called mountains by the locals), green forests, quaint roads, and a number of smaller towns or villages. Many of the roads had first been used in colonial days, with their courses little changed since Indians and settlers had walked along them. Navigating through this part of new Jersey is interesting, because there were few signs marking town limits, and every town had a universal set of road names, and of course, none of the road names of one town lines up with those of the adjacent settlement. It paid to be patient and travel in daylight. Murray Hill could be reached by following the quaint roads through Scotch Plains, Summit, and New Providence for a distance of six to ten miles from the motel. We found and cased Murray Hill and its' immediate surroundings after we found our motel, and had been impressed with the massive Bell Laboratories operation.

    The Bell Labs Headquarters, located at 600 Mountain Avenue, Murray Hill, resembled an insane asylum plopped down in a small, forested, well-groomed golf course. From the front, two very large six-story brick buildings were evident, each holding several thousand technical people, and to the west, sat a detached building housing an auditorium. The main buildings, numbered one and two (right to left), had elevator shafts protruding from the roofs that looked like guard or machinegun towers, thus contributing to the appearance of an asylum or possibly a medium security prison. There was no security fence; otherwise, the illusion would have been complete. The extensive well-groomed grounds included a three-hole golf course, shuffleboard, bocce, and tennis courts, so one wondered if the inmates were from the wealthy classes. Administrative Building 3 was not visible from Mountain Avenue, nor was additional support facilities and the huge parking lots stretching out east, south, and west of the main buildings. I did not realize it at the time, but none of the buildings were air-conditioned. There was also a dress code. Unlike NEL in San Diego, at Bell Labs it was expected that slacks and dress shirt would be worn. I think that neckties were encouraged but optional. I would find that the combination was not very comfortable in July and August. Fortunately, a Vice President, Bill Hettinger, eventually showed up for work wearing Bermuda shorts, and the summer dress code essentially disappeared. However hot or sultry, it was <u>never</u> ok to be sloppy or disheveled.

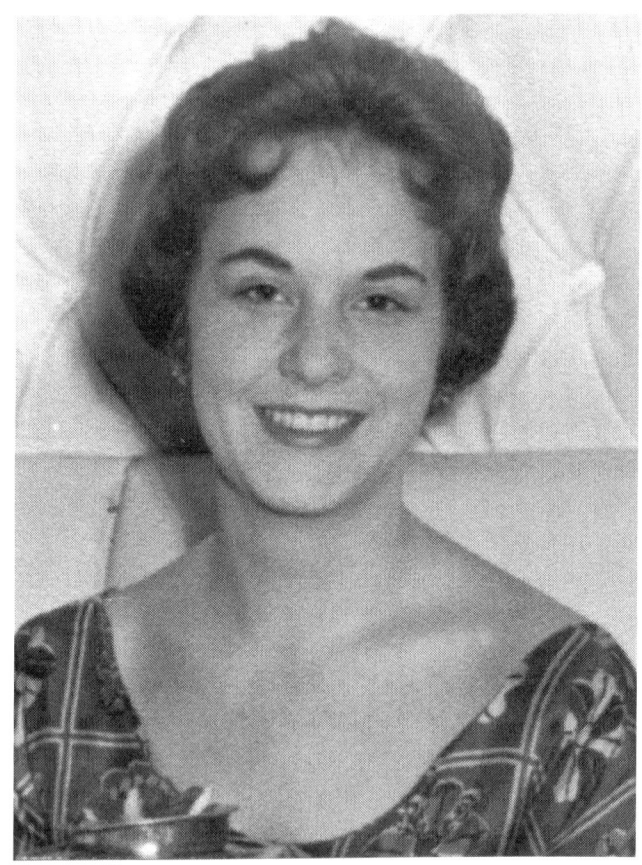

Judy, My First Wife, - early 60's

My Earliest Experiences With the Personnel Department at BTL

When Judy and I drove to the Labs to report in, we first drove to the main entrance in one of the "guarded" structures, Building 1 I think, but we were directed to Building 3, the large square administrative facility on the south side of Building 1, away from Mountain Avenue. I was warmly welcomed aboard by the personnel people, who were apparently tasked with making me feel like a member of my new very extended family. I filled out various forms, signed my name several times, and was given the employee number 049620. I filled out an expense voucher covering the cost of our travel from the west coast expecting some complaint for the amount of my requested reimbursement. The personnel man frowned, and handed it back to me saying, "It is not possible to get to Murray Hill from San Diego for such little money! You must have made a mistake!" He told me to correct the tabulation and left the room. His efforts to get me to increase the dollar value of my voucher were to no avail. I had not been trained in account padding, not even with friendly assistance and patient urging. He muttered something like, "As an employee of Bell Labs, you must uphold high standards, and behave accordingly". In the future, I would try to fix this character flaw with some success. I don't remember the details, but eventually Judy took the car and she went off to look for more permanent quarters.

I had been hired as a "Member of Technical Staff" or simply MTS, and would be enrolled in "Communication Development Training" or CDT for short. As part of my quick indoctrination, I learned that at Bell Labs titles like "Doctor", "Professor", "Sir", and "technician" were never to be used. Coworkers were to be addressed by their names, regardless of their achievements or position in the pecking order. I was naturally suspicious of authority, had learned to yell at my superiors at NEL, and now I was **required** to call them by name like ordinary citizens. That struck me as just fine! How democratic!

The CDT program consisted of courses taught by staff from New York University and by distinguished Bell Labs MTS. The coursework included Information Theory, Numerical Methods, various advanced math courses, and some training in Bell System History and Practices. The material sounded interesting, but since the program took over two years to complete, I was a little discouraged regarding balancing CDT coursework with technical work demands. I wished to excel in both. As it turned out I did eventually do well at both but it was touch and go for quite awhile. I felt fairly sure I would earn my princely (it seemed at the time) salary of around $900 per month.

The CDT program involved not only additional schooling; it also involved multiple work assignments. The program was begun with me working in a temporary "home" group, followed by three additional rotational departments, followed by possible return to the home department. I don't recall whether it was intended for the last assignment to be permanent, but at the time, I didn't care. I would later care a lot, but for now, I simply wanted to get on with things. The exciting world of new knowledge beckoned!

I was shown the location of all the important facilities, such as the bathrooms, cafeteria, library, stockrooms, and most importantly, I was introduced to Ed Walsh, my new immediate boss. Ed in turn showed me my new home, laboratory 2B209, and introduced me to some of my new compatriots. These included Director Jim Early, Head Brian Howard, Head Eric Iwersen, fellow MTS Carl Martersteck, Ed Nicolian, Martin Lepselter, Rudy Schmidt, and Joe Ashner. I met many others as well, but as usual, their names faded quickly from my brain. Ed Walsh's group was working on device packaging and reliability issues. I was told to make myself at home, and invited to familiarize myself with the work of the group.

My first real disappointment with the situation came when it sank in that starting almost immediately, the initial CDT course loomed. Worse, the graduate level material in the first course was normally covered in full three semester-hours, but now we were going to do it in about six weeks! I was also under the impression that I was expected to begin contributing at my home department. Ed made this point very clear. I don't remember the subject material of this first course, but the conditions were not good. The temperature was in the nineties, the facilities were not air-conditioned, the humidity was high, and we were living in a motel. I stayed up late at night studying, and I caught a very nasty summer cold while sleeping under the window air conditioner. Time passed really quickly, and after a while, I got an "A" in the course. The grade was good, but I had contributed nothing on the job, and in addition, I was a physical wreck. My supervisor, Ed Walsh, noted the grade, but said little of the accomplishment. I assumed that here, excellence was the norm. There would be more grades to comment on in the future.

47 Dogwood Lane, a Really Nice Place For Kids

Judy found a nice split-level house to rent, located at 47 Dogwood Lane, just about a mile from BTL. The rent was a little expensive, but we both thought that it could be managed. It was to later turn out that we really couldn't manage the financial burden, but this simple fact took awhile to become **painfully apparent**. This was particularly true because I was almost totally absorbed in work and the associated schooling. I didn't want to be bothered with simple worldly matters such as rent or other small details such as bills.

The house was located on the eastern, curved side of Dogwood Lane, a short, quiet D-shaped road. The interior of the D consisted of common unfenced back yards and so formed a perfect playground. The setting was almost perfect. There were many fair-sized trees and a lot of green grass. The only traffic was local, and the economic status of the local inhabitants seemed roughly in line with our own. Soon the moving truck arrived with our meager belongings, and the Kerrigans drove out from Des Moines with the kids. Our little family was together again, and we looked forward to our new adventure.

We met our new neighbors next door to the north, Bob and Mrs. Harney. Two Canadian couples, the Dicks and the Holmes, lived on the opposite (western) side of the Dogwood D. Both the Dicks and the Holmes would become good friends in the years ahead. I had no lawn mower so the Harneys loaned me a rotary mower to keep our weeds in check until I could buy one of my own. I eventually bought a mower on sale from Bamberger's for the grand sum of $50. I was to use this lawn mower into the late 70's before it finally expired. Each of the Canadian couples had children with ages close to ours. The neighborhood kids had free reign of the back yards, and the low traffic density in the surrounding roads reduced any fears regarding dangerous traffic.

One aspect of this part of New Jersey was the high water table. Our rental house was a split-level, and so had no water problems. The Holmes house had a basement, and their experience was a little different. The Holmes wanted to smooth the floor and walls before refinishing it. They discovered that only a thin layer of sealant was preventing massive leaking from the water standing just outside their basement walls. I don't recall just how they solved the problem, but we would later experience the joy of water problems when we eventually moved to Walton Avenue, nearer to the Passaic River.

Study, Study, Study, and Maybe a Little Work

I don't really remember the details of the coursework, but I recall that I had courses in "Numerical Methods", "Information Theory - Random Signals and Noise", "Digital Logic", "Statistics and Probability", "Number Theory and Advanced Calculus", "Dimensional Analysis and Similarity", and a course named something like, "Bell System History and

Practices", to round me out. Somewhere along the line, we briefly studied patent matters, and the importance of maintaining a well-written and adequately witnessed notebook. There may have been other courses, but these are all that I can recall.

Numerical Methods introduced us to the use of finite difference equations and techniques in the solution of complex physical problems. Here the analytic methods developed in earlier times fall short, because measurements do not form a smooth continuum, but are instead discrete quantities, and because of the discrete nature of digital computing. Dr. Hamming, a well-known mathematician and Bell Labs MTS, taught the course. He was both instructive and entertaining. In one lecture, while we were discussing the power and limitations of digital techniques as applied to periodic or repeating functions, he observed that, "For years I tried to apply these techniques to my wife's menstrual cycle, and in the end, I could only say that if she was late one cycle, it was likely she would be early the next". He also warned us as to the folly of applying these methods to other cyclic phenomena such as the stock market. It was too easy to generate false correlations and projections. As I write this in 2010, this admonition is still appropriate. It is very hard to tell how much of the Climate computer simulations yield results just realistic enough to be believable.

Number Theory and Advanced Calculus fascinated me. Two professors from New York University (NYU) taught this course. They were writing a textbook on the material as they taught it, so there was no textbook. At the outset, the axioms were stated, and theorems were rigorously proved as we proceeded. We began with integers, and then proceeded through irrational and complex numbers, proving **all** deductions as needed, <u>without exception</u>! The progress was slow but easily followed, because nothing was left as an exercise for the unwary (or lazy) reader. We then moved on to calculus. I had already taken three calculus courses, but this was like being on a new world. We moved through the material in exactly the same way as the work with number theory. In fact, this work used all we had learned about number theory. **No** unproven theorems were left undone throughout the material covered. I had fared well in my earlier math courses, but in those courses the emphasis was on mechanics or manipulation, and many of the crucial proofs had been left "to more advanced work". Here, we had crossed an enormous chasm, and a solid stone was always underfoot. What a difference! I was elated! I kept copious excellent notes written in bright green ink, because no textbook was available, and I wanted to be able to refer to the material in the future.

I recall little of the course on probability theory, but I do remember that concepts learned in this course were to stand me in good stead throughout the rest of my work in semiconductors. In particular, I learned the power of **probability paper** when analyzing data. **Probability paper** features a vertical axis upon which the value of the desired variable (or some function of the variable) is plotted, while the horizontal axis plots the cumulative probability of each value entered on the vertical axis. If the plotted variable is distributed in a "normal" manner, then the resultant plot is a straight line, inferring a simple population. If the plot consists of more than one straight-line segment, the inference is that multiple populations representing different mechanisms are present. If the plot does not result in straight line segments, than the phenomenon is not "normal", and may not be random. This type of analysis was to be particularly useful when I was part of a massive effort called "Phase 2", and later on when I worked at Teletype Corporation in Skokie IL, and later still when I was advising Lithographers in the Western Electric DRAM line in Lee's Summit, Missouri.

In "History and Practices of the Bell System", I learned the Bell side of early patent battles between Alexander

Graham Bell and Elisha Grey, the importance of early business leaders to the formation of our Bell System, and other items of interest to employees and historians. I also learned about various key technical developments in the communication world, such as coaxial lines, microwaves, invention of the transistor, and creation of the first electronic central office switching systems. I also learned that having been a lineman was a key qualification for a person to rise to the top in AT&T, a sobering thought. The course was short on technology but at least we learned the company song, and possibly the company salute and cheer. Recall that in those days, Bell Telephone Labs was arguably the transcendent industrial technical organization in the United States, possibly in the free world.

Dimensional Analysis and Similarity was an extremely interesting topic. I don't know that I ever really used formal dimensional analysis, but the concepts were useful in slightly other guises.

Taco, or - Four More Feet Join our Family

I don't recall just when we decided to expand our family, but on one cold weekend, we traveled to a kennel in northern New Jersey, and selected a small furry companion as an additional mouth to care for, feed, clean up after, and so forth. As I recall, we thought that the dog was part

Chihuahua, and part a small terrier. Because we were recently from Southern California, to honor his heritage, we named the critter "Taco". Taco would turn out to be an excellent dog. Getting him housetrained was of course no fun, but he soon learned his role, and Judy and I were soon convinced that our quality of life had definitely improved. From my own point of view, the worst part of the deal was having to take the dog for his walk on cold winter mornings and evenings, while holding on to his string, just like the numerous other dog owners in the area.

During his puppy-hood, he did not eat our furniture, as had another dog we knew, and only occasionally destroyed a stray shoe that had been carelessly left for his enjoyment. Otherwise, his upbringing was fairly easy and painless. Like all terriers, he was a great watchdog. He would suitably growl at the slightest nocturnal noise. He also liked to growl at other critters, and would strain at his leash or against a window to get at another animal that happened to come into view.

When he was still quite young, Judy brought home a set of Easter ducklings, that she quickly named, "Penny Rude", "Rudy Whistle", "Mamie Hustle", and another that I can no longer remember. Taco still slept in the garage, because we were still unsure of his toilet restraint. Pending construction of a small outdoor pen, the ducklings were momentarily put into a tall box inside the garage for the evening. As expected, Taco heard the ducklings and reacted by barking and much growling, straining vigorously to get to the quacking little critters. We had temporarily restrained Taco with his leash, and went to bed thinking that all the garage inhabitants would survive the night.

Next morning, before the coffee had finished perking, no sounds emanated from the garage. Hoping for the best and fearing the worst, we opened the inside garage door to find the ducklings either sleeping on or snuggled into Taco. Apparently, the ducks had gotten out during the night and they had all made friends. It was a really cute sight. He was a really good dog, as might be expected. Eventually we would place the ducks in a wildlife refuge when they grew larger. Ducks do not make good pets in an urban surrounding.

A black and white cat that I named Fu Manchu would eventually join us some five or so years hence, when we lived in Allentown, Pennsylvania. Fu Manchu would lead me to understand what I called **"the Cat Pee Syndrome"**. I'll say more about Fu Manchu and the **Cat Pee Syndrome** later on, in Chapter 6.

A Little Work

When I was not in class, I was in my room, eating lunch, in the library, or talking with other members of the department to get a better understanding of the ongoing work. The class work was time consuming and occupied much of my mental energy. Nonetheless, Ed had indicated that he expected me to participate in the work of his group to the best of my ability. The group had a job to do, I was part of his team, and he gently encouraged me to get on with it. It was not difficult for me to learn more about the ongoing work, but I soon noted that as I walked into a lab to talk to the resident worker, any open Laboratory Notebook was quickly closed and any visible notes tucked carefully away. It soon became apparent that the competitive nature of the Laboratory did not encourage teamwork. There was a general fear among the technical people that their own precious ideas would be pirated, and the originator's identity lost forever. "Friendly", "reserved" and "uncomfortable" were words that described many of these encounters.

2B209, my personal laboratory, had windows facing east and was located on the second floor in the northeastern wing of the "B" section of Building 2. This wing is located around a quarter mile from the main entrance that was near the cafeteria, and over a half mile from Building 3, where the

CDT courses were taught. I was to occupy this lab until I was transferred to Allentown in 1965 five years hence, as well as when I returned to Murray Hill still as an MTS in 1971. I circulated freely among members of the group, became aware of various aspects of their work, met many other people, and attended many local seminars. Later on, I would begin to play chess, both with other lab members after hours, and after lunch at the game lounge situated just above an entrance to the cafeteria. It was during this time that I first met and became friends with George Richards. George was an excellent chess player, and we would also play chess once a week at his home in Summit, where he lived with his wife. Rudy Schmidt would eventually join in these friendly chess sessions.

My brother, Wilson E. (Buddy) Waggener Jr. and family, had moved to Madison Wisconsin, where he worked for the Prestressed Concrete Products Corporation in Verona. Buddy and wife Katharine had been busy, and in September, their third child, Carol Sue was born. Buddy was practicing his Architectural Engineering profession and was enjoying his work. His geographic location would be problematic for us, because our location severely limited our ability to make more than one trip back to the Midwest per year.

Chapter 2 - My First Work Assignment 1961-1963

Find the Balls of Solder!

Ed had suggested that I work with Joe Ashner, a metallurgist who was working on the problem of making electrical connection to semiconductor devices using "solder balls". In those days, individual devices were fabricated in regular arrays on a thin silicon wafer, cut into individual chips by sawing with a diamond saw or by scribing, then individually mounted onto a package base, device-side up. Thin wires were then attached to allow electrical connection between the device terminals and the package leads. The solder ball technique, first introduced by IBM, was intended to simplify the packaging. The Bell System had developed precision thin film resistor technology formed on ceramic substrates, and these inverted devices were potentially a real step forward. There were two main problems with solder balls: First, the materials and conditions had to be carefully chosen to avoid cracking of the brittle silicon due to thermal expansion-induced mechanical forces, and second, the need to easily accomplish alignment between the leads on the substrate and the device. It was necessary to align pad areas on the die with corresponding areas on the substrate and then press them together prior to melting the solder. Silicon is metallic gray in appearance and looks metallic when viewed in visible light. In the alignment operation, the die was upside down, and the substrate is an opaque ceramic, so that mating pad areas were hidden and not directly visible.

A Happy Coincidence - Infrared Alignment

By chance, I attended a talk in Arnold Auditorium, part of our complex, given by Spitzer and Fan, two BTL scientists who lectured on the optical properties of silicon. They described how silicon, while opaque in visible light, was transparent in the infrared region. Bingo! It occurred to me that if indeed silicon was as transparent as glass in the infrared, then the use of an infrared image converter should enable easy alignment of upside down die onto a substrate pattern. I went in search of an infrared image converter, and was led to the lair of Barry Cohen[1], who was working on gallium arsenide devices, and who coincidentally had a homemade infrared (IR) microscope using a commercial RCA image tube. Barry loaned the microscope to me, and I proceeded to apply it to the alignment problem. It worked! Ed Walsh was impressed with this minor breakthrough, and told me to continue the good work. I was to buy several more image converters, and adapted them to various existing equipment for my purposes.

Ironing out the details of applying infrared to the alignment problem was to occupy me for some time. The first problem was that it was essential to have the backside of the silicon polished, so that a good image, not a mere crude shadow, could be seen. Second, it was highly desirable to arranging the lighting so as to get as much light under the die as possible. This involved intense side lighting. Third and more troubling, the silicon tended of to become opaque during the alignment process. It turned out that the illumination lamp would heat the silicon, which led to a dramatic reduction in light transmission. The heating in turn was dependent upon the conductivity of the silicon die material. Heavily doped

---

[1] Shortly after this, Barry went to Israel on a leave of absence. When he returned to the USA, he began to manufacture IR microscopes in his garage. Some twenty-odd years later, He would be my Glorious Leader at Lepton Inc. That is another story.

material was affected more. Thus, it was necessary to tailor the surface smoothness and light source location and illumination wavelength to minimize heating effects.

A Fatal Error in Procedure, not Easily Overcome

I was sandwiching my CDT courses with my work assignment, so the continuity of effort was compromised. Nonetheless, I was able to characterize the effects of silicon conductivity and light source properties into a manageable and useful form, and painfully wrote a draft in the format of the chief internal publication, a **Technical Memorandum or TM.** I hand wrote the TM, sent the result to the secretarial pool for typing and after my own review, joyfully sent it to Ed Walsh for comment prior to dissemination. Ed marked a number of corrections, and sent it back for change. Therein began a vicious cycle. I had always been proud of my literary ability, so I was dismayed with the faults found in the document, and delayed reworking it. Worse, when I finally did rework it, a painful process of physical cut-and paste, I mistakenly sent the revised text again to Ed for further review. It once more came back with <u>new</u> markups! This cycle was repeated several times before I finally gave up entirely. The tattered and faded memo eventually sank to the lowest layer in my right-hand bottom drawer, and I refused to work on it further. Ed did not recognize the nature of the problem, and the fact that I had originated the work was soon lost on the technical community at large.

The fatal error was a result of my lack of training as to the real procedure to follow, and an overwhelming desire to be perceived as competent. I confused Ed's markups as disapprovals, not as editorial imperatives. **If I had simply fixed the first revisions, and issued the resulting text in a TM, all would have been well.** The written information would have made it into other peoples hands, everyone would have been pleased, and my rating would have benefited greatly. Instead, I became so discouraged at the ordeal of publication that I retreated from writing up or recording my work. **I relied instead on personal communication and an informal network of coworkers. This was a near-fatal flaw in my development as an outstanding technical contributor!** The remnants of this experience dogged me for a number of years. At Bell, as in many other scientific organizations, an important but often unstated motto was **"Publish or Perish".** My development was severely damaged, but I eventually made a modest recovery. The comment was, **"He does excellent work, but never writes it up"!**

Telstar - The First Communication Satellite - 1962

In the fall of 1960, AT&T Bell Labs had begun the development of the famed Telstar communications satellite. Telstar was intended to blaze a new path in telecommunications technology and insure that AT&T would get a jump on the competition. The development schedule was very short and the effort was intense.

I really would have liked to have been part of the project but I did not become directly involved. I did get to know some of the people who did. Brian Howard was one of my early interviewers, and his group was in the thick of working on devices for the satellite. The Van Allen belt had been discovered earlier, so that any devices to be flown needed to be able to tolerate very high levels of radiation, a tall order, since detailed knowledge of the underlying physics was poorly understood. Using a Cobalt 60 radiation source, device structures, fabrication and packaging combinations were tested for longevity until useful combinations were found. I did not contribute to this work except as an interested spectator.

The Telstar design relied on solar cells to power the satellite. In 1954, Bell Labs scientists had invented silicon solar cells, and the people involved believed that they could develop a design that would be adequate for the purpose. My Director, James M. (Jim) Early is credited with designing the transistors and solar cells used on the satellite. These devices not only had to withstand the intense light of the sun unfiltered by the earth's atmosphere, they also had to withstand the radiation of the Van Allen belt and repeated cycles of high and low temperatures encountered as the satellite rotated in space. The device design also required a novel metallization scheme. Martin P. Lepselter developed the metallization scheme. I was to become a close personal friend and coworker of Martin (Marty) in the near future. I still have a number of the original solar cells left over from the Telstar project, and after forty plus years they still are as good as new.

Another significant innovation was the development of a high efficiency high power klystron vacuum tube to power the satellite transmitter. The group responsible for developing this device was located on the first floor of Building 2, one floor below me in the same wing of the building. I would meet them in the future, when they took me under their wing at the IEDM meeting in Washington, DC.

Almost a year after I arrived, Telstar 1 was flown successfully on July 10 1962, lifted into an elliptical orbit by a NASA Delta rocket. The spherically shaped satellite weighed 171 pounds, and the new newly developed Traveling Wave

Transmitter (TWT) and the receiving equipment provided bandwidth of some number of voice channels or one TV channel, as compared to only a few voice circuits available via the underwater cable telephone circuits then available between Europe and the United States. A hydrogen thermonuclear device was exploded in space by another arm of our government just hours before the flight of Telstar 1, and the massive radiation released caused some device malfunction, but the experiment performed according to expectations. There was also a clear need for better coordination between government agencies.

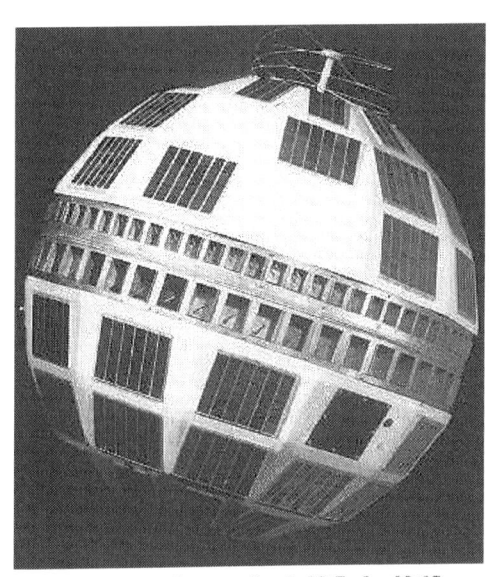

Telstar 1 - Launched 10 July 1962
The first of 18 eventually launched. [2]

---

[2] Photo taken from http://en.wikipedia.org/wiki/Telstar.

Telstar 1 was a stellar (no pun) success. A second Telstar satellite was successfully launched, but the bid to dominate the satellite business ended when in the early sixties, President Kennedy issued a policy statement that avoided the possibility of a Bell System Satellite monopoly.

The Bell System continued to be a force in space efforts, at least in part due to it's historical role in the surface-to-air missiles dating from near the end of the Second World War. In addition to the satellites, ground-to-air- defense missiles and planning for space missions were to be features of AT&T's efforts for a number of years.

In 1963, AT&T set up a subsidiary of the Bell System called Bellcomm Inc., located in Washington DC, to assist in the planning of space activities. Brian Howard and Karl E. Martersteck were transferred to Bellcomm some time after I arrived at Bell, but I had some time to get to know Karl. Bellcomm was very involved with planning of the Apollo program. A year or two later, I visited Karl at his office in Washington, and he showed me a three-dimensional model of the lunar surface where the Apollo lunar landings were planned. I don't recall whether this meeting occurred before or after the lunar landing/spacewalk actually occurred. Karl would eventually become a Vice President of Bell Labs after he returned to the Bell System proper.

The Nike Surface to Air Missile Systems and Case Charges

The Bell System was deeply involved in work related to space and national defense. The Western Electric Company, an AT&T subsidiary, was the prime contractor for a surface-to-air Missile (SAM), the Nike Ajax. Development of the Ajax missile had begun in 1947 when I was in grade school, and the development activity continued into the mid 1960s. I believe that another version, the Nike Hercules, had also been developed. By 1958, many Nike batteries were deployed in defense-critical sites and were in active service. When I arrived at Bell Labs, the Nike Zeus, a newer third-generation form of the Nike missile was being developed, and in September 1961, the first successful full three-stage flight occurred. Alas, I was not involved directly in any of these projects, but the background thinking that had evolved within Bell had a profound influence on my future technical work.

Nike Ajax, designed to bring down
bombers at altitudes up to 60,000 ft. [3]

Any of my work that was associated with space activities was strictly peripheral in nature. We charged our work time to several cases, so that the various projects in which we were involved would be properly accounted for. The words behind the case structure had been written quite independently of the MTS, and it was never clear to me what specific case I was working on at any given instant, except for my CDT block of time. Thus, when I worked on infrared alignment, some of the overall work might have been actually

---

[3] http://en.wikipedia.org/wiki/Nike_Rocket

funded under a military case. My managers had the responsibility of insuring that our time was properly assigned. Similarly, shop work and materials were charged to various cases. In this instance, the guidelines were **absolutely** clear. Use Bell System cases except for instances where it is absolutely obvious that a military case is appropriate. If auditors discovered an inappropriate charge on a military case, termination would be immediate, with no recourse. That seemed unambiguous enough.

I continued my CDT work, and at the end of a full semester received all A's, the highest grade available, and was contributing positively on the job, with the limitations described above. I liked the coursework, but also wanted to contribute more effectively on the job. After all, I had come here to compete with the best of the best, and I was still in a parking orbit. Or was it the parking lot? I feared the latter and worked for the best outcome I could manage.

A Christmas Party I Didn't Attend

I was not aware of it at the time, but apparently, the Department held a Christmas party this year. Although Judy and I did not attend, I heard later that it was held at some large restaurant that included an area suitable for presentation of a play. After Dinner, various members of staff presented a skit lampooning both their supervisors and Bell Labs in general.

The skit describes a supposed incident in the Nike Zeus anti-intercontinental missile development program.

> *The scene opens with a group of supervisors huddled around the instrumentation in the Nike missile control center on Kwajelein, in the Pacific Ocean. There is a planned test of Nike about to start. For this test, it has been planned to launch an ICBM with a dummy warhead in the general direction of San Francisco, and a Nike is to be launched from Kwajelein to intercept and shoot the ICBM down in mid-flight.*
>
> *The ICBM has just been fired, when they get the word that at the last minute, the parameters of the test have been slightly changed: The ICBM has been armed with a live nuclear warhead, and has been retargeted directly toward San Francisco!*
>
> *There is considerable jabber and frenzy by the supervisors to launch the NIKE. Shortly thereafter, a stunned silence falls over the group when telemetry shows that the intercept has failed!*

One of them speaks: "Well, we have lost a NIKE, worth several hundred million dollars, an ICBM worth even more, and San Francisco will doubtless be destroyed! But don't worry, our jobs are secure, because at least we didn't compromise a mail girl!"

I wasn't at the party, but that is what I heard about it. Perhaps the skit gave some insight into the existing culture.

My First (Almost) Merit Review - 1962

At some time during the first year, my boss, Ed Walsh, ran across me in my lab, and said, "I have heard nothing negative about you, and a few good things. I guess that you will receive a small raise this year. You will need to work harder to retain your ranking in the future." and Ed then walked away. This was less than encouraging to me, since I had been told that my starting salary was based upon a "first octile rating", meaning that I was in the upper one-eighth of my classification. The first octile rating matched my internal expectation and ego, and anything less than that would have registered as a defeat. The effect upon me of the almost-review was nagging disappointment. It was like having to check to see if your fly is open or if there is a booger on your nose when people seem to avert their eyes from you when you first enter a room. In short, it was a letdown.

I did not realize it at the time, but Bell Labs management really put a lot of effort into the merit ranking process even though at least some individual supervisors were poor in presenting the results to their charges. When Bell Labs was initially formed in facilities located on West Street in New York City, the founders had to eventually face up to how to distribute money to the employees. Upon reflection, they decided that it was fairly easy to divide any group of employees into those better than the local average and those below the local average. They further decided that this process could be applied twice more, until the whole population was divided into eight levels, or octiles. The most highly rated employees were placed in octile one, and the most poorly rated employees were placed in the eighth or bottom octile. The founders considered that further subdivision was futile. They also instituted the notion of Job Titles, from stockroom clerk to President.

As the organization grew and the nature of jobs and locations multiplied, the beauty of the simple system disappeared. Each Job Title was independently scored, and while different organizations maintained the same Job Titles, they often changed the associated requirements. In addition, it soon became apparent that different locations needed to receive different pay for identical Titles because of wide cost-of-living differences. It was somewhat like in a George Orwell novel, "All pigs are equal, but some pigs are more equal than others". There was also the problem of attracting new employees, and fitting them into the existing pay scale. Bell Labs was noted for high technical achievement, **not** for high salaries. This latter problem was at the root of my consternation. The situation became extremely confusing to many, and was frankly a source of much employee distrust and unrest.

    The rating-morale problem had become so acute that management had developed a slick compilation of data called the "Green Book" which I eventually came to believe accurately compiled the company-wide data into a compact form. Unfortunately, while it was possible for an individual to tell where he stood on a company-wide basis, either by job title, by time out of school, or with an "x" or "y" degree and so on, <u>it was impossible to tell how you were ranked with respect to your local peers.</u> Not only that, but it was widely believed by the troops that the Green Book data was rigged or somehow falsified. Thus, much of the hard work and good intention of the company was wasted, and many employees were confused and unhappy because of it. After all, we all believed that we were hired because we were among the best, and needed considerable reinforcement. Egos are hard to suppress without good data.

A grass roots group distributed questionnaires relative to salary particulars. The form was anonymously sent in for independent analysis by unprejudiced or at least less interested parties. I don't remember what this salary survey was called, but a lot of work seemed to be put into it. As I said, many people didn't trust the Green Book, and looked to this analysis for meaningful interpretation.

Some things To Do, Or Not

There were few formal rules concerning conduct or behavior, but it was generally accepted that dress shirts and slacks were appropriate attire, with a tie desirable but optional, unlike our counterparts at IBM. Starting times were announced, but no one paid attention to your detailed hours of attendance. It was assumed that performance trumped attendance. I have already indicated that one of the cardinal sins was to inappropriately charge material or shop work to a military case. I also found that there were other causes for dismissal. One sure fatal infraction was to be too personal with a mail girl, who were all of high school age, and so were strictly off limits by rule. Stealing or gross dishonesty could also result in being summarily walked out the door. Another cause for dismissal was to be found bringing or keeping alcoholic beverages on the premises.

Within my first year, I knew someone who was walked off the premises for an infraction of the mail girl rule, but that first Christmas, I found a curious modification to the absolute ban on alcohol. One day as I was walking on the first floor of building 2, one level below my lab, I thought I smelled a badly overheated power transformer or other electrical device, and I looked for the source of the smell. I discovered a small party, where they were serving a delicious concoction, "Glueg Wine". The department responsible for the Telstar traveling wave tube (TWT) development was having a departmental Christmas party, and had temporarily suspended the no-alcohol rule. The drink was both delicious and relaxing. I would meet these people again under other circumstances at my first International Electron Device Meeting (IEDM) in Washington DC. I'll say more about that later.

Interestingly enough, if it was determined that a relatively new MTS was lacking in performance, the individual would be quietly invited to find another job outside Bell Labs within some time limit, but no comment was ever made as to why someone had left the organization. It was said however, that when someone left for such a cause, the intelligence level of both groups invariably increased as a result. Being famous was no defense. Performance commensurate with the salary level and hiring position were absolutely necessary to remain part of this elite corps. I eventually came to understand that many well-known individuals were thus recycled back into the technical community. In time, I knew several such people, a few pretty well.

YMCA Indian Guides, and a Delaware River Canoe Trip

Sometime around this time, Judy and I met Marge and Earl Lanning and their three kids. Both Marge and Earl were educators. Marge taught in grade school, and Earl was a principal at a nearby school. These were very personable and likeable people, and our families became good friends. They fit right in with the Dick and Holmes families, and we often gathered together to party. Earl also was associated with a YMCA organization known as the Indian Guides. Earl suggested that this would be a good program for Mark, John and I to join, and we did. The Indian Guides was a little like the scouts, but the emphasis was on father-son bonding. Only father-son pairs could participate. At that time, there was no equivalent program for fathers and daughters. We were duly inducted into the Wasatch Nation and we assumed Indian names. I was named "Big Thunder", Mark was named "Little Thunder", and John became "Lightning Quick".

The individual Indian Guide Lodges met either biweekly or monthly, and meetings consisted of solemn recitations and craft activities, held in our homes on a rotating basis. Once a year, a great tribal meeting was held at a YMCA camp, where we all slept in rough facilities, and lived a little like Indians (?) for a few days.

Another activity our local tribe engaged in was overnight canoe trips on the Delaware River. We would rent canoes, put them atop our cars, and travel to Port Jervis NY, just north of the New Jersey state line. At Port Jervis, we put our canoes in the water, having carefully loaded them with plenty of beer for the men and plenty of soda for the boys. After about three or four hours of paddling downriver from Port Jervis, we encountered a small island, where we stopped and set up camp. We would string up a canvas canopy, and feed ourselves. At nightfall, we would just talk and tell stories before going to bed in sleeping bags.

In the morning, we would rekindle our campfire, eat breakfast, and prepare to take to our canoes again. Just before we left, we would let the boys put out the fire. It was a good way to empty their bladders before the final leg of our journey. After a few hours, we would reach Dingmans' Bridge, a location used in colonial times, and carry out canoes to a waiting car we had previously left there. We would get back home before dark, tired, hungry, and well satisfied. I felt that the weekend had been well spent, and I was ready for further adventures in semiconductors.

Vacations are to be Scheduled in July

Bell Labs had strict policies regarding taking vacations. It was understood that many of the staff were compulsive workers, and I was told that management strongly advised each employee not to take vacations a day or two at a time, but rather to take at least one week as a block annually, preferably for two consecutive weeks, if possible. It was considered absolutely necessary to allow the mental batteries to recharge at least once a year. I don't recall whether July was a suggested month for vacations due to plant facility maintenance, or not, but in any case, July was to become our standard vacation interval.

During our scheduled vacations, we had a significant trip to make. We would typically take vacation in the Midwest, driving first to Des Moines Iowa, and then on to Lakeside, Missouri in order to visit both sets of Grandparents. The trips were always a challenge. There were three parts to the challenge. First was the distance. The total round trip distance was around 2,800 miles, which at an average speed of 50 (?) miles/hour was 56 hours. Fifty-six hours is a long time to be cooped up in a car under any conditions. We had little money, so that motel stops would be limited at best, and typically of poor quality. Worst of all was the heat. Our early cars did not have air conditioning, so the heat and the wind noise from the open windows were almost overwhelming.

We considered the discomfort well worth the price, because we got to see our loved ones once more. I treasured these times, in spite of the trauma. I'm not sure that the kids agreed, but they had little choice in the matter. In a few years, Judy's sister Anne would live in Chicago, so we could stop there on the trip out. The stop at Anne's improved that leg of the trip considerably.

CDT Is Completed, But Am I Finished? - June 1963

I completed the CDT part of my training in two years, and received an impressive "Bell Telephone Laboratories Certificate" testifying as to my completion the "Communications Development Training Program" dated 27 June 1963. I got A's in every class. I don't think that this was unusual, but it seemed to impress Ed Walsh and Jim Early, the director of my home department. Ed and Jim were to soon interview me, and both commented favorably on my outstanding coursework.

> **BELL TELEPHONE LABORATORIES**
>
> THIS CERTIFICATE IS AWARDED TO
>
> *H. A. Waggener*
>
> IN RECOGNITION OF HIS SATISFACTORY COMPLETION OF THE
>
> **COMMUNICATIONS DEVELOPMENT TRAINING PROGRAM**
>
> *June 27, 1963*
>
> *Frank D. Learner*
> Executive Director, Personnel Division
>
> *John N. Shive*
> Director, Education and Training
>
> *J. D. Such*
> Head, Training Department

Either one or both of them pointed out that because of this success, my capabilities were eminently clear, and that from now on, a great deal would be expected of me. Unbeknownst to me what they were telegraphing was to expect declining ratings, because my initial first octile ranking was an artifact of hiring, not an indication of my current or future real worth to the company. Had they told me the truth, perhaps I would have been much happier in the next few years. Again, I did not realize that Department Heads, Directors, Nobel Laureates, and the like inhabited the top octile. Thus, it would have made sense to me that I would

67

have to fight extremely hard (or be damn lucky) to achieve such a rarified rating.

I Attend my First IEEE International Device Meeting

My home department was involved in silicon integrated circuit work, and Ed suggested that I attend the 1962 IEEE International Electron Device Meeting (IEDM) meeting then held annually in Washington DC. This meeting and the later IEEE International Solid State Circuits Conference (ISSCC) were two of the **must-attend** conferences in our field. I took the shuttle flight to Washington, a taxi to the Washington Hilton where the conference was held, and checked in. I don't recall whether I arrived Sunday night or later on. The conference was scheduled to last several days, and the sessions were chock full of interesting stuff! I was an avid attendee and was almost whelmed by the flood of information. A standard feature of the meeting was a Wednesday evening cocktail party where free booze and 'hors d'oeuvres were served. The intent was to encourage interpersonal communications and to help form new thought patterns. Quite naturally, I helped myself and soon was quite relaxed as were many others of the hundreds of attendees. Wine, cheese, and fruit were much in evidence, and the bar served whatever you wanted, no charge. I met Jim Early and saw a few others that I recognized, but the place was awash with strange faces, all swilling their favorite beverage as they renewed old acquaintances, as was the plan.

After a couple of hours, the crowd began to thin out, as various groups formed and went off to have dinner, more drink, and more talk, probably in that order. I suddenly found myself standing almost alone, as the few people in my department had gone. I was feeling left out, when the people from the first floor Glueg party spotted me and asked me to join them. I was happy to be included, and readily accepted the offer.

The group had chosen to go to a Spanish restaurant named "El Bodegon" not far from the hotel. When we arrived, the place was bustling. A group of patrons was waiting to be seated, but the wait seemed short and worthwhile as smiling customers continued to stream out of the place. Our group totaled perhaps 15 or 20 people or so and we were seated in a small alcove on the second floor. The group ordered food for me, since I had no idea what the items on the menu tasted like. We also ordered Spanish wine that was served in a container called a bodegon, the glass equivalent of a Spanish wine skin.

A Bodegon Acquired from El Bodegon, Washington DC, displayed on our deck at Lake Wissota WI.

The wine container was designed to dispense wine in a stream. To obtain a drink, you had to open your mouth, tilt your head back, and let the wine stream into your mouth, without spilling any of the precious nectar on your clothing, napkin, or table, and without letting the container touch your face. We practiced this procedure enough to get it down pat.

Eventually the Flamenco dancer came to entertain us. A small wooden platform was brought into the alcove, followed by an Irish guitarist, the owner of the restaurant, and a good-looking female Flamenco dancer strutted her stuff.

Their performance and the wine made for a most enjoyable meal. After the entertainment went to another part of the restaurant, the waiters encouraged us to be more adventuresome with the wine. The challenge was to begin streaming wine as before, but now letting the little rivulet fall on your face, then up the outside of your nose, further yet onto the forehead and back into your mouth again. An important object of this game was to drink without spilling any wine in the process and making a mess of oneself. After a few hours at El Bodegon we were full, <u>very</u> relaxed, and some of us were still actually dry. We walked back to the hotel together, and I went to my room to sleep the sleep of a Zombie. The next day I was back the conference absorbed in the technical sessions. I don't know how I managed to fit the conference into my school schedule, but I did.

Thus, I had been properly indoctrinated as to the expected behavior at these conferences. This meeting became the pattern for meeting attendance for the future. I always tried to hold up my end of the festivities. This was a great opportunity to make new friends and technical contacts. Better yet, Bell Labs paid for everything, and they wanted us to go first class. I made it a point to neither gain or to loose money on these occasions.

During this interval, it became painfully apparent that we could not afford the rented house on Dogwood Lane. In my single-minded zeal to succeed at Bell Labs, I had failed to notice the state of out finances. There were two problems. A first indication was the need to repay a small loan to my Uncle, Dr. Robert Clark. Repayment of the note took precedence over my attending Sister Suzanne's wedding held in Kansas City Missouri on 4 November 1961.

Suzanne and Mary Waggener getting ready for Suzanne's wedding to Thomas Mower.

Suzanne Wedding Photo - my beautiful sister!

Married in Kansas City

Miss Susanne Waggener, daughter of Mr. and Mrs. Wilson Evan Waggener of Joplin, became the bride of Eugene Thomas Mower of Kansas City at a ceremony at 2 o'clock Saturday afternoon, November 4, in Central Methodist church in Kansas City. The ceremony was read by the Rev. Ray McCliskey before a background of white and tangerine carnations.

Given in marriage by her father the bride wore a gown of white taffeta styled with basque bodice and a slightly scooped neckline highlighted with Chantilly lace motifs centered with sequins and pearls. The long tissue taffeta sleeves tapered to points. The skirt was accented at the front with inverted pleats and the back swept into a chapel-length train detailed with three fishtail tucks. She carried a cascade of white roses and stephanotis.

Miss Barbara Nan English of Lawrence, Kan., was maid of honor. Miss Nancy White of Dodge City, Kan., was bridesmaid. They wore ballerina dresses of satin and velvet in beige and brown fashioned with basque bodices, scoop necklines and elbow-length sleeves. The full gathered skirts were accented at the back of the waistline with designers roses. They wore brown satin pillbox hats with matching circular veils.

Richard L. Reinking of Lawrence, Kan., was best man. John M. Tyler of Tulsa was groomsman and Jack Black of Topeka and Gary Cordell of Kansas City were ushers.

Following the ceremony, a reception was held in the Bellerive hotel. Janet Atkinson was in charge of the guest book. The bride's mother wore a brown satin gown with beige accessories and corsage of miniature yellow roses.

The couple will be at home at 1320 East Eighty-ninth street in Kansas City.—(Forest E. Miller photograph).

4 NOV 61

A second later event, was even more telling. I was alerted to this difficulty by a sheriff calling on me at Bell Labs during business hours to bring my attention to the matter. The nature of the problem was not discussed with the kids, but we soon moved to a smaller, less expensive place located at 100 Walton Avenue, also located in New Providence, only a little further away from work. I'll have more to tell about this place later on in the story.

First Rotation - My Niobium Tin (non) Superconductors

This assignment took me out of the component division, where the emphasis was on applied research to the Research Division. I was assigned to work with Robert Sinclair, an excellent metallurgist in Area 1, the basic research organization. Bob had laboratories in a building called "The Elephant House", located just behind building 2, only about a half block away from my lab. When I first entered Bob's lair, I found him standing with his head and shoulders inside a large glass bell jar that he had swung around from the vacuum system so that he had access to it. I announced myself, and asked him, "What are you doing"? "I'm cleaning out the deposits on the inside of this bell jar", he replied, his voice sounding hollow and a little distant. "What is that smell"? I asked, wrinkling my nose and making a sour face. "Trichlorethylene", he replied, as he looked through the bell jar at me. Trying to look unconcerned, I asked, "How can you stand the smell? Won't that stuff eat your liver and kill you?" I knew full well that this use of the offensive chemical had been banned a few years before. When he had finished his tasks, he exited the bell jar, and explained to me that his olfactory organs had been damaged years before in connection with experiments involving elemental fluorine, so he was no longer bothered by chemical odors, and that he figured that he was old enough that he was relatively insensitive to limited exposures to low-order toxins. I looked at him and could only shrug my shoulders.

From that instant on, I felt that I was to become The Sorcerer's Apprentice, not an **apprentice physicist.** Thus, we began a long-term friendship, as I tried to make a superconducting film under his guidance.

High temperature superconductivity, beginning at around 17 degrees Kelvin, had been recently found in samples of the bulk intermetallic compound Nb_3Sn (pronounced "niobium three tin"). Bob thought that it would be a great scoop if we could discover superconductivity in thin films of the compound. Bob had most of the needed components, including the vacuum system, the bell jar of which he had so recently cleaned. Whatever else we needed was either ordered or fabricated in the adjacent machine shops. With little delay, I was depositing films on glass substrates, attempting to create films of Nb_3Sn. The films I deposited were analyzed as to composition and structure by other coworkers with Bob introducing them to me as needed.

When measurements showed that we had about the correct chemical composition, we rigged an electrical measurement system that could cool the samples to below liquid helium temperature while monitoring the sample resistance. No signs of superconductivity could be found. The plot of resistivity vs. temperature showed not even a suggestion of a wiggle as we passed 17 degrees Kelvin, the temperature where bulk samples of Nb_3Sn became superconducting. It was apparent that either the films were too full of contaminants, or that the structure simply was not correct. It soon became apparent that extensive modifications would have to be made to the deposition apparatus in order to have even a remote chance of success, but that would take us well beyond the scope intended for the rotation process.

The work was interesting and I learned a bit about superconductivity, more about vacuum equipment, and a bit about cryogenics. I had a great time, but the effort was not a success. I decided not to write up the failure, which in retrospect might have been yet another grave mistake, but I was still numbed by the Ed Walsh incidents, and did not realize that I was shooting myself in the foot. On the positive side, I had learned how not to clean bell jars!

Second Rotation - Thin Film Technology - 1963

I don't know how these things were arranged, but my next rotation exposed me to the fabrication of thin film resistors and capacitors. The substrates used to make these devices were in fact the kind of units to which I had earlier applied an infrared microscope to align upside-down devices. At that time, much of the Bell system was analog in nature. The oxide masking process had been invented at Bell Labs in 1954, integrated circuits at Texas instruments in 1958, and planar technology at Fairchild in 1959. Planar technology resulted in what was known as monolithic integrated circuits. These early integrated circuits all used bipolar transistors, where the essential parts of the transistor is controlled by the details of the materials buried deep inside the bulk material. The monolithic format allowed complex integrated circuits to be fabricated, and the industry was off to the races.

In 1961, the digital revolution was underway, but had only barely begun. Discrete transistors were still used to implement logic functions where the highest speed performance was needed. The Bell System business included a great deal of voice messaging in both local and long distance services. Circuit designs were incorporating transistor gain elements, but the precision resistors then needed for narrow band filters were not easily achieved in silicon. Thin film technology had been developed at Bell for producing precision resistor and capacitor networks on glass and glass-ceramic substrates. These networks made possible the tone generation and detection circuits used in the first touch-tone phones, thereby making rotary dial telephones obsolete.

The Bell Thin Film Technology used deposited tantalum or tantalum nitride films, which were subsequently patterned to form resistors and capacitor areas, followed by conversion of part of the thickness of the metal into an oxide film by a process called anodization. I knew nothing about anodization, but soon learned that certain metals could be immersed in a suitable ionic solution, and that by connecting the metal to a positive voltage in a simple cell, an insulating oxide film could be grown. I did not know it then, but the knowledge I gained concerning electrically driven oxidation of metals was critical for my later development of a revolutionary silicon etching technology in 1969.

MTS like me who were on rotational assignments were sort of like summer employees. They could only be involved in short-term projects. When I arrived in the thin film area, I met R. W. "Bob" Berry, B. L. Kennedy, Murray Harris, and several others. I was welcomed into the lab, and given a simple task of interest to my management and other workers in the field. They asked the question, "When tantalum is anodically oxidized, does the oxide film grow by tantalum ions or oxygen ions moving through the growing oxide film"? The subject had been the object of considerable debate, and they thought that the question could be easily answered experimentally.

They proposed that I anodically oxidize double layers of tantalum/aluminum and aluminum/tantalum sandwiches and by etching off the oxide layers so formed, determine which ion was moving through the growing film. Since the chemical properties of the oxides were drastically different, the determination as to which oxide was formed on the outer surface would be easy. I was happy to do the work. I quickly set up the equipment, and performed the etching experiments. The results were unequivocal.

If aluminum metal had been originally on the outside, after anodizing through the aluminum, tantalum oxide formed at the outer surface! Similarly, if tantalum was the outer metal, after anodizing through the tantalum, aluminum oxide was formed on the outer surface! These films grew by metallic ions moving through the oxide films under the influence of the applied fields.

ECS, Pittsburgh PA –My First Talk - 1963

The experimental results were excellent and dramatic. R. W Berry, B. L. Kennedy, and I wrote an abstract for a talk to be given at the next Electrochemical Society meeting. I presented the talk, "An Investigation of the Diffusing Species in the Anodic Growth of Tantalum and Aluminum Oxides," at the spring 1963 Electrochemical Society meeting in Pittsburgh Pennsylvania. The talk was well received. I knew the subject well, and had something to say.

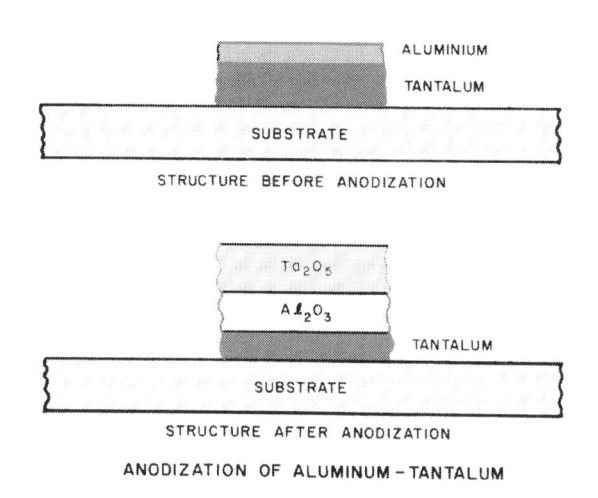

Structure before anodization: Aluminium layer on top of Tantalum, on Substrate.

Structure after anodization: Ta_2O_5 on Al_2O_3 on Tantalum, on Substrate.

ANODIZATION OF ALUMINUM – TANTALUM

Later that year, I realized that anodization of dual layer metal structures could result in resistors and capacitors with **very** superior stability compared to current practices. The instability of anodized resistors was partly due to the fact that tantalum oxide was soluble in tantalum metal when heated, while aluminum oxide was not. Thus, the incorporation of an internal aluminum oxide layer should result in more stable resistors. Bob Berry agreed, and Murray Harris continued to work on the proof of principle.

Anodized tantalum before and after
650-700°C for half hour.
Very Large Color Change

Anodized tantalum-aluminum before
and after 650-700°C for half hour.
Virtually No Color Change
The underlying tantalum is protected by Al2O3.

Murray performed two main kinds of experiments. The first was to demonstrate the overall thermal stability. Anodized tantalum dissolves the anodized oxide when heated, and the color of the film changes accordingly. As the above pictures show, temperatures as high as 650 to 700 degrees Centigrade resulted in little color change for the composite films! He next performed voltage-step-stressing of both protected and unprotected resistors, far above their normal working limits. This also demonstrated much lower resistance change with stress, as indicated on the next page:

RESISTANCE CHANGE WITH ACCELERATED POWER AGING

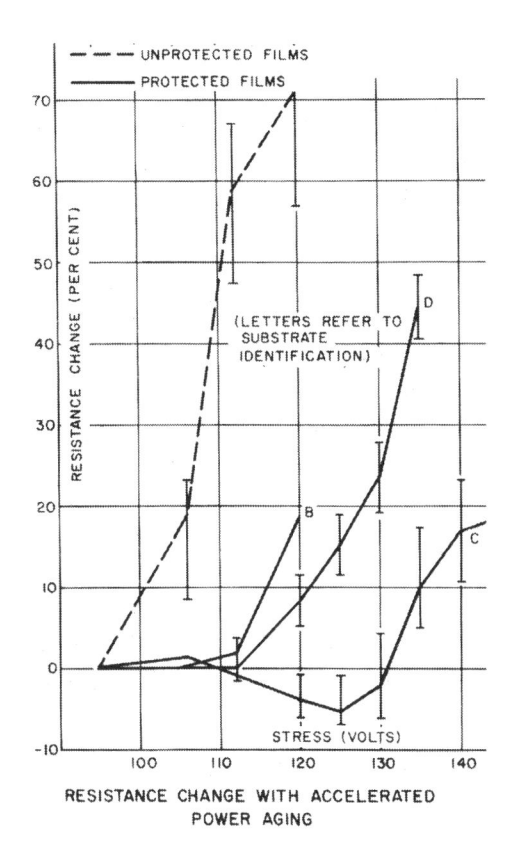

The protected resistors exhibited much better stability than the normal, unprotected devices. We issued a joint memorandum in January 1964, and wrote up a patent application, starting the patent process. In October of 1964, a patent was filed. Patent # 3,457,146 was finally granted on 22 July 1969.

I was to later find out that the process was never accepted for production, because the devices incorporating aluminum oxide could not be adjusted to the final value by the hot air trimming techniques then in use on the production lines. Once formed, the devices made using the new structure were simply too stable to trim. Thus, the technique was not exploited in-house. Nonetheless, my management recognized my contribution, as did I.

Following my exposure to (maybe) superconductors and thin films, I returned to the world of semiconductor technology to work in a department headed by J. E. (Eric) Iwersen. This would be my third and last rotation. Jack Morton, Vice President of the components division, was convinced that the role of integrated circuits would be self-limited to what he called **"right-scale integration"**. He was convinced that chip sizes would be limited to around 40 to 50 thousandths of an inch square, and worse, the circuit speeds would always be inherently slower than circuits that were constructed of individually fabricated and selected devices arrayed on a suitable substrate connected by individual thin gold or aluminum wires. Iwersen's department was charged with working out ways to improve the performance and reliability of silicon integrated circuits. It was evident to many of the troops that Morton was dead wrong on all counts, but it would take a while for the truth to emerge.

100 Walton Avenue, Smaller and Cheaper

Walton Avenue is located somewhat nearer the Passaic River, in an area where the homes generally were a bit smaller than those on Dogwood Lane. The house was a small New England cottage style (cracker box), with a finished second story and an unfinished basement. We all noticed that the pattern imbedded into the kitchen floor covering had the appearance of spilled food, with scrambled eggs, mashed green peas and various bits of miscellaneous stuff readily imaginable. The place was definitely a step down, but the much lower rent gave us needed financial relief and helped us attain some monetary breathing room.

One of our first construction activities was to build a patio in our back yard. Before we could begin the patio construction, several large stones needed to be moved. It was a warm summer day, when dressed in t-shirt and shorts, I picked up the first large rock to move it out of the way. The rock was quite heavy, and to lift it, I rested my forearms on my knees to support the weight. About the time that the rock came to rest, I noticed that there was a dense swarm of angry hornets attacking my bare legs.

Apparently, I had disturbed the hornet's lair, and they were letting me know that they were resentful, in no uncertain terms. Well, I normally react quickly to bad situations, but what was I to do? I could not throw the rock, because it was too damn heavy to throw. I could not drop the rock, because it would crush at least one of my feet. All I could do was gently put the rock down a little distance from where I had gotten it, and get the hell out of the area. Fortunately, I was not highly allergic to the stings, because I had gotten dozens of stings, and the leg swelled to only twice its normal size. I don't recall that I sought medical assistance, but walking was a problem for a while.

John, Mark, and Shawn, Walton Avenue, New Providence NJ 1964

Our Munchkins - Mark, John, and Shawn - 1964

While we rented there, we partitioned and finished the basement, with the landlord gladly furnishing the materials. We already knew that this region was prone to a high water table, from our knowledge of the Holmes experience. We also knew that a house a little further down Walton Avenue had severe cracking of their foundation due to high water pressures on the walls. Inspection of our little basement revealed no seeping water or cracking foundation walls. There was a sump pump in one corner of the basement that seemed to keep the interior quite dry. The basement had an exterior entrance with heavy exterior steel doors and an interior wooden door. We would soon find that frozen ground could interfere with operation of the sump pump, a critical component.

**Aunt Rose, Uncle Atkin, Herb, Mom and Dad Waggener
Walton Avenue, New Providence - 1966**

Karen Johnson was a girlhood friend of Judy's, who had gone to Stephens College at the same time, and who had been a bridesmaid at our wedding as well. Karen was working in New York as a dancer while keeping herself alive as a waitress. One day in late winter/early spring, she visited us at Walton Avenue. There had previously been a heavy snowfall, and the snow was one to two feet deep all around the rear (north) of the house, and that afternoon a gentle rain began falling. We had planned a small celebration, when we realized that there was a problem n the basement.

When we discovered the problem, water was about one stair deep and rising! Apparently, the outlet of the sump pump was frozen solid out near the street, and worse; the snow had formed a natural funnel for the rain to run directly into the basement through the crack in the outer cellar door. The combination was deadly. Our basement made a lovely wading pool. Fortunately, only rainwater was involved, with no mud or sewage to befoul the walls and floors. Unfortunately, all of my carefully taken notes from the CDT courses were lost along with some books, and possibly some other things as well.

I think that either the landlord or the fire department finally arrived with an auxiliary pump to empty the basement. I don't recall how the frozen outlet line was thawed, or the problem otherwise addressed, but soon the basement dried out and was useable again. My precious notes and books were not so lucky.

I Build a Superb FM Stereo Receiver After Hours

As a MTS, I had full and complete access to the numerous Stock Rooms. The stock contained a plethora of electrical, mechanical and office goodies. We were encouraged to use the stock rooms as we saw fit, but we were asked not to supply our friends and neighbors with Bell Labs Material. It had come to the attention of Jack Morton that the stock rooms were being used as a hiring inducement. Jack wanted the practice to STOP! RIGHT NOW! After a few days, supervision came around and "interpreted" the Morton Memorandum. The only change in direction would to be a stronger policy regarding supplying others, and a prod to make certain that whatever we built with Bell Parts would be a learning experience. I discussed the situation with Eric Iwerson, and he said that building a receiver sounded like a learning experience to him! With this clarification, I designed and built a first rate FM Stereo Receiver to complement the preamp and power amplifier I had built in San Diego.

I wanted to have a very low noise, high gain system, and I designed it accordingly. I built the high frequency parts of my receiver in three sub-chassis interconnected by coaxial wires to minimize the possibility of unwanted oscillations. Each sub-chassis was made of copper, and the first (input) chassis was gold plated to reduce high frequency skin effects. I salvaged the tuning capacitors from my Heathkit, and built the first stage using very high gain miniature vacuum tubes called nuvistors, operating in what is called a cascode arrangement. Nuvistors™ were built using technology that had been invented for undersea cable applications, and were the very best devices then commercially available. The stereo decoder and buffer amplifier were built on a fourth flat copper sheet, and everything was mounted in a custom-built aluminum master chassis. I hand bent and assembled each copper box, and painted the aluminum master chassis black.

Using the original Heathkit dial as a template, I scribed a new dial in plastic and mounted pulleys and other materials behind a newly fabricated brass faceplate. The finished receiver looked really great, and it worked like a charm! I still have the receiver in 2010.

Scratch-built FM Stereo Reciever in Case for Shelf Mounting
The receiver used a lot of watts, but was really excellent.
The left knob is a dummy. On-off was part of the preamp.

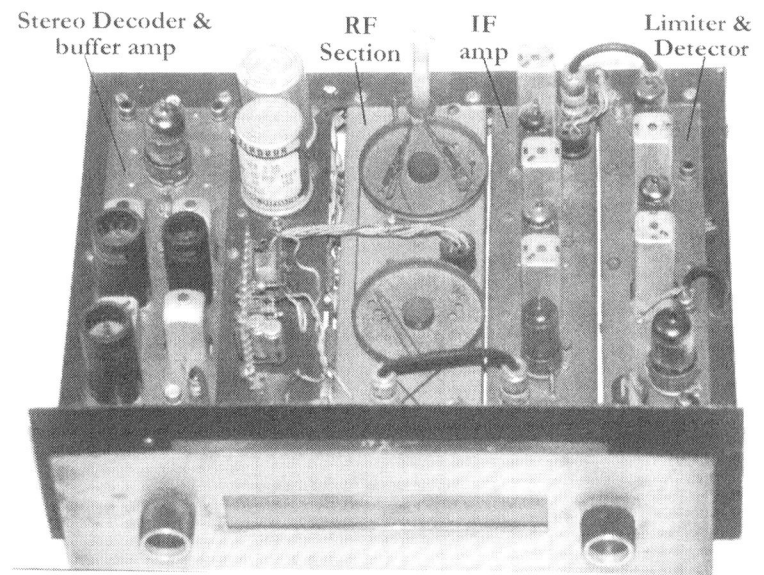

Top view of HAW scratch-built FM Stereo Receiver

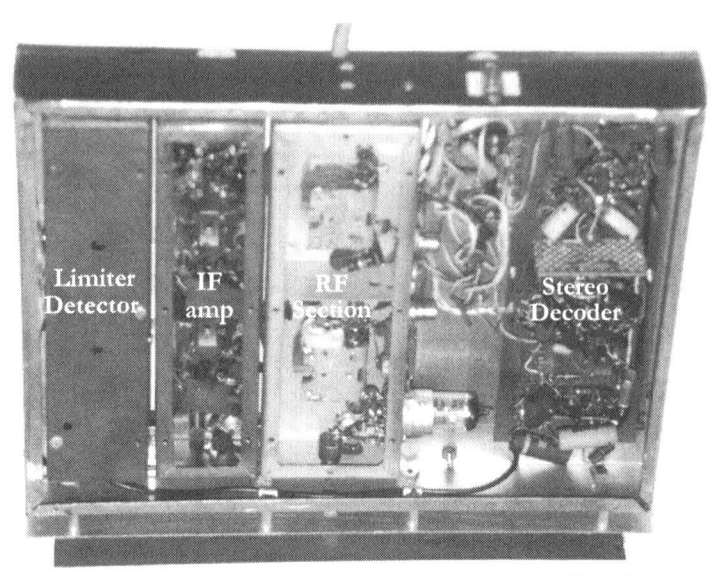

Bottom view of HAW scratch-built FM Stereo Receiver

I used this receiver for many years, until it was finally replaced with commercial equipment in the 80's.

During this time, another directive came down from Jack Morton stating that integrated circuit technology was no longer a suitable subject for development in Murray Hill, and that anyone working in this area should find something to do in areas that are more important. Many people knew that he was wrong, but few would challenge his authority. As my local management and I were checking both our options and our shorts, someone convinced Morton that the effort should not be aborted so suddenly, and a new amended directive came down shortly. Perhaps there were yet diamonds to glean in this area. Breathing a collective sigh of relief, those still present picked up where we had left off.

There was yet another row concerning the inappropriate use of the stockrooms. This time the problem was the inordinate number of withdrawals of mechanical pencils and other office supplies. I don't recall the particulars, but we were admonished to cut back our mechanical pencil[4] use. It was said that in Murray Hill alone we had checked out enough pencils to equip every individual in the immediate residential area with at least six or more pencils. The directive certainly had a salutatory effect on our use of such implements. It seemed particularly odd that such a matter would be brought to our attention. Here were some of the more technically creative people in the world, being told to conserve on pencils. Go figure, no pun intended.

---

[4] A Bell System mechanical pencil fetched from my archives. The color of this one is light blue, but dark green was also used

93

My Second (or Third) IEEE IEDM

Attendance at the annual IEDM was considered mandatory. On this occasion, Eric Iwerson, who was to become my department head, and I arrived late Sunday night for the meeting, and all the usual rooms were filled. The only rooms available were sumptuous suites, which were normally rented for several thousand dollars a day. We were issued such a suite for the standard convention rate of around a hundred dollars per night. When we walked into the foyer of the suite, saw that there was a large reception area, a living area, a large kitchen and dining room, and there were two large bedrooms with individual baths. Eric's comment was "If we had any sense, we'd throw a party for everyone". I don't recall any details of the meeting, except that once again, I consumed my share of the refreshments at the cocktail party, and as would become standard practice, I dined at El Bodegon.

In these days it was commonplace to make devices on tiny pieces of silicon, usually less than one half inch per side. Often broken or irregular fragments of silicon as small as 3/16 inch would be processed to completion. Material quality was poor, surface quality was poor, and quality control in our experimental facilities was nonexistent. It was a marvelous time for clever experimenters. Almost everything was an improvement over previous art. I was thrilled with the area. It was apparent that semiconductor technology would revolutionize modern life, in ways that could not yet even be imagined. It was great to be part of this overarching technology development. **_Perhaps here I could make a footprint in the sands of time_**.

An image printed for me on a 4 in x 5 in x 1/4 in reticle blank by the Murray Hill Mask Shop expressing my work philosophy. I tried really hard.

Chapter 3 - Semiconductors

Some Integrated Circuit Problems Needing Solution for AT&T Systems

The highest priority guiding the components division was the reliability of devices used in our system products. The main business of AT&T was the services provided to customers, and the revenues thereby gathered. AT&T had a very large investment in it's network facilities, including undersea cables, copper lines, radio carrier systems, and switching centers, all involving vacuum tubes and semiconductor devices in various degrees. It was the intent of the company to provide extremely reliable service as a part of their promise to customers. Reliable devices provided improved service by reducing downtime, network degradation, and expensive repairs. The more calls per unit time the facilities could reliably handle, the greater the economic returns. Thus, very high reliability and device performance were dual goals.

Performance Limitations of Early Bipolar Integrated Circuits

There were many problems influencing performance-that needed solution in these early days of bipolar circuits, and various people both inside and outside the lab were working on them all. Performance limitations were primarily of two kinds: The size of devices, and parasitic resistances and capacitances arising from the fabrication processes then available. At that time, the only technology was bipolar. MOS devices had been invented, but were not yet reliable enough to be useful to us.

It was well known that the performance of a bipolar transistor depended critically on the device dimensions, both lateral and vertical. Lateral geometries were limited by the ability to print small features using the existing photographic techniques. This was also a primary limitation for MOS devices. Existing photo alignment/exposure tools were rudimentary, and the photosensitive materials needed to print and etch the lateral device geometries were crude. Then as now, there was a lot of effort in the industry to improve the exposure tools so that smaller devices could be made. Rudy Schmidt, a German engineer used a microscope operated in reverse to print very fine device patterns, and was able to make devices with record breaking capabilities, foretelling what was to come.

The vertical geometries that could be achieved were much smaller than the lateral features. The critical vertical geometry was the width of the transistor base, formed by first forming a base diffusion of different doping type than the starting material, followed by a shallower emitter diffusion of the opposite conductivity type, nested inside the base region. The electrical base width was determined by the difference in depth of the base and emitter, and this dimension could be made much, much thinner than that attainable by the lithography then available. As the base width became small, defects tended to create shorts between emitter and base, thus limiting the base width practically achievable. Rudy and others worked hard to minimize these problems.

Parasitic resistances and capacitances surrounding the device caused a further performance limit. One such resistance was a result of the physical distance needed between the region under the emitter and the collector contact. Another important parasitic was capacitance associated with the junctions that were diffused into the structure to isolate individual circuits (prior to base and emitter formation) from each other where needed by circuit design. A third performance limitation that had reliability implications was the simple electrical resistance of both the interconnecting leads and the regions where aluminum made contact to silicon. Other problems would arise later on.

Reliability and Cost, Reliability and Cost

There were several reliability problems common to silicon devices of that time. Aluminum was the industry standard for the internal metallization. Aluminum could corrode, fail at high currents, penetrate junctions when hot, and could interact and fracture where they contacted the gold wires used to connect the semiconductor die to the leads on the packages. It was also discovered that device reliability was worse for hermetically encapsulated devices than it was for unsealed devices.

The packages themselves could also be unreliable. Connection to the die could be erratic, and under some conditions, the package could develop leaks, the leads could corrode, or be difficult to solder into circuit boards.

In addition to the performance and reliability issues, packaging was expensive, because each operation had to be performed individually. Part of the economy of integrated circuits lies in the fact that many circuits are made simultaneously on each wafer, and for many steps, many wafers can be processed together. When a wafer was completed however, the situation changed. Individual die were cut or broken from the wafer, and each individual good die was bonded to substrates, and each wire connecting the die terminals to the package were individually bonded in place. This "back end processing" resulted in the expenditure of many man-hours in the final assembly and test area. Martin P. Lepselter, a brilliant Brooklyn boy, invented Beam Leads and thereby sidestepped many of these problems.

Martin Lepselter Conceives Beam Leads

Martin Lepselter invented a device structure in 1964 that neatly sidestepped several of the performance, assembly, and reliability problems. Marty invented a new metallization and packaging system called beam leads. In this technology, the single metal aluminum was replaced with a composite three-component metallization system. In effect, the complexity added by the beam lead approach was offset by the resulting economy of self-packaged devices. The device side steps needed to accomplish this are listed on the next page.

1. Deposit a layer of platinum on the wafer after contact windows are formed, and heat to an elevated temperature to allow platinum silicide to form in the contact windows.
2. Etch the wafer in aqua regia to remove unreacted platinum, leaving the platinum silicide in the contact windows.
3. Deposit layers of titanium and platinum over all.
4. Use photolithography to define and electroplate thin gold, forming the complete metallization pattern.
5. Use an additional photolithography step to define the thick gold electroplating to form eventual beam interconnections to the outside world.
6. Remove photo-resist, and remove exposed platinum and titanium using plated gold interconnections as a self-aligned mask.
7. Expose the beam leads by removing silicon from under the beam leads from the reverse or backside of the wafer.

The net result of the steps outlined above was an array of self-leaded devices, waiting to be tested, picked up, and bonded directly to appropriate substrates for use. Thus, expensive attachment of individual leads was avoided, and in addition, aluminum-gold reactions at the chip level were altogether absent. Internal reliability failures of the metallization were avoided because of the additional electrical and chemical stability of the beam lead metallization scheme. As an aside, Jack Morton reviewed Lepselter's early work and when he viewed the gold plating bath used to form the beam leads he asked, "What is that, a urinal?" indicating a possible lack of interest. He did not seem to recognize that this would represent the start of both MEMS and MMIC technology[5] of today.

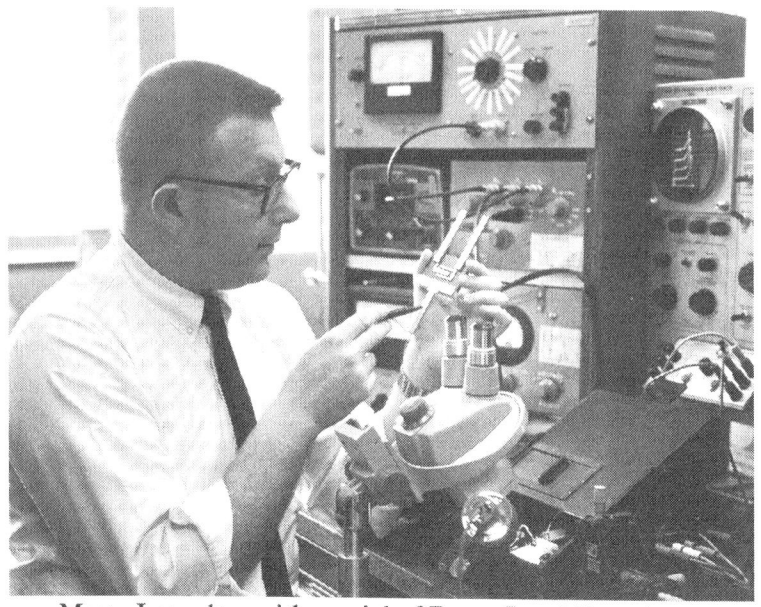

Marty Lepselter with model of Beam Lead Transistor
at Bell Labs Office in 1965

---

[5] MEMS stands for Micro Electro Mechanical System, and MMIC stands for Monolithic Microwave Integrated Circuit.

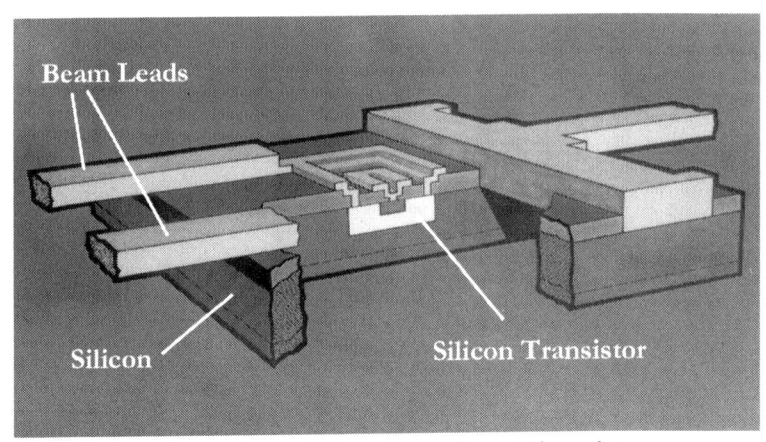

Cutaway view of First Beam Lead Transistor
The beams were 1 - 2 mills wide, and 1 mill thick.
The silicon thickness was 2 mills.

Third Rotation - Integrated Circuits Again - 1964

Enter Herbert Waggener stage left. Eric Iwersen assigned me the task of finding better ways to thin the silicon and remove the material under the beams, both essential steps in the beam lead approach, particularly for structures more complex than simple devices. Silicon is brittle. Wafers used to fabricate devices are made thick enough to permit handling for processing without breaking. For the wafer diameters then in use, the starting wafer thickness was about 0.008 inch (about one fourth the thickness of a human hair).

In order to make completed beam-leaded devices several steps were needed as indicated in step 7 above. While the concepts were simple and relatively straightforward for simple transistors, for more complex structures, the devil was in the details. A viable technology had to be scalable to production, and depended critically upon simple economics. We needed to make the process simple, cheap, and robust. The basic steps needed to convert finished devices into beam leaded chips are outlined below.

1. The beam leaded wafer was mounted onto a flat sapphire disc with wax, making sure the beams and sapphire were in close contact.
2. The silicon had to be thinned by either chemical or mechanical means to a thickness of around 0.002 inch.
3. The mounted and thinned wafer was coated with thick photosensitive etch-resistant material that was resistant to the next silicon etchant.
4. A front-to-back alignment and exposure was performed to place the backside-etching mask of step 3 so as to protect the desired device areas.
5. The silicon underneath the beams was chemically etched away in a hydrofluoric acid-nitric acid etchant to expose the bottom side of the beams, and the etch-masking material removed.
6. The devices were electrically tested-in-place for proper functionality.

7. The good devices were removed and cleaned, making them ready for direct attachment to a suitable circuit.
8. The devices were bonded to the circuit board using heat and localized pressure on the beams. All necessary beam lead chips were individually placed and bonded onto the substrate until all devices were in their proper places on the desired circuit substrate.
9. The completed substrate might again be tested to insure functionality, and repaired if necessary.
10. The bonded devices were buried under a blob of silicone rubber to provide mechanical protection, making the substrate suitable for its intended use.

When making devices in this way, it is necessary to **not** have the etching process intersect the device junctions and thereby ruin the device electrical characteristics. When the first beam lead devices were made, the etchants used to remove the silicon from the wafer backside to expose the beam leads were composed of water, nitric, and hydrofluoric acids. These etchants were isotropic, meaning that they etch silicon at a uniform rate in all directions, as illustrated on the next page. In the drawing, the etching proceeds with a rate, R, measured from the edge of the etch mask, so that the etch distance, r, is given by r = R x time.

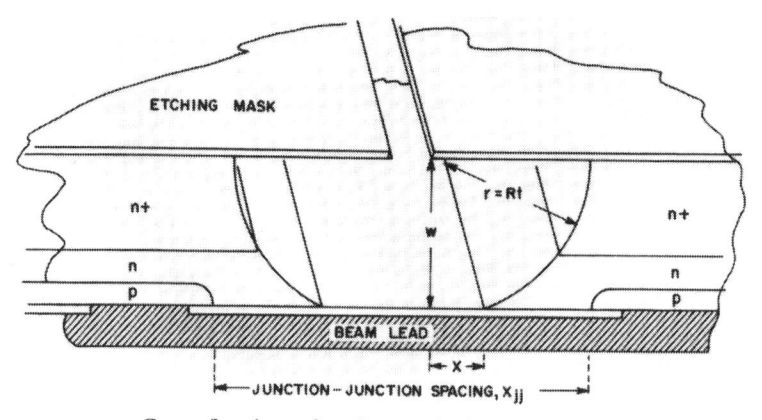

Cross Section of an Isotropically Etched Slot
The slot geometry, thickness and alignment variation requires large junction spacings for high yield.

The isotropic etching procedure was simple, but a large area was required to get adequate yields, so I would soon look for other means for removing the silicon.

I got involved with the beam lead activity very early on. I outfitted my infrared microscope to an Electroglas alignment system for proper placement and exposure of the backside mask. The alignment system had to be modified to enable a light source to be placed under the wafer. I don't recall whether this was done in-house or by the vendor of the machine, but I was having fun! I was operating as a member of a team of Lepselter, R. W. MacDonald, R. E. Davis and myself, and the many people involved in the model shop, including Mike Tomsky and Delbert Deppen.

Beam lead transistors fabricated by R. W. MacDonald and R. E. Davis were shown to be extremely reliable at high temperature and they also survived salt-water corrosion tests that would have destroyed any commercial device in seconds. When bonded to a substrate, the devices were capable of withstanding loads in excess of 135,000 times the force of gravity or G's, the limit of our centrifuge. Eric Iwersen was dubious about the concept but changed his mind when he picked up a tiny string of microscopic transistors with tweezers, and was **unable** to cause them to bend by rapid hand and wrist motions. The fact that he could generate only a few G's in this way did not seem to be of any importance. He had bought into the concept.

Early AIM Technology Development, Murray Hill

While the device reliability testing was in progress, I immediately began to work on applying beam leads to the problem of reducing unwanted electrical parasitics associated with the junctions then used to provide electrical isolation within integrated circuits. I named such air isolated monolithic integrated circuits an **"Isolith"** (**Iso**lated mono**lith**).

Eric soon pointed out that the prefix iso and base lith were from different languages, and therefore inappropriate[6] to combine. Even so, several companies in the industry described their own versions of this high performance technology as Isoliths. I typically referred to them simply as **AIM** (Air Isolated Monolith) devices. Several years later still, I was to later develop a form of air isolation without beam leads, so I started calling these earlier types **B**eam **L**ead **A**ir **I**solated **M**onoliths or simply **BLAIMs** for short.

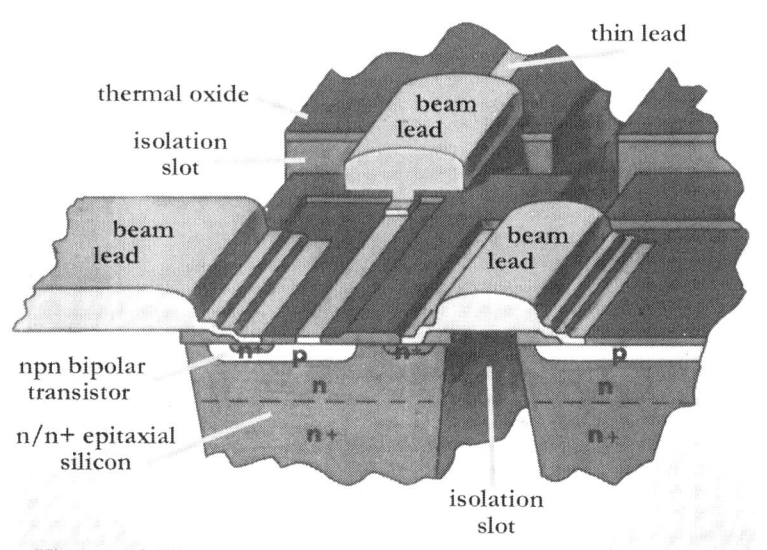

Viewgraph Illustrating Elements of Isolithic Integrated Circuit

For me, the problem was how to form accurately placed, very narrow physical slots between devices within each integrated circuit while removing the silicon from

---

[6] The people at Sylvania marketed such devices as "Isyliths".

109

underneath the beams from the backside. Beam leads on the device side would hold the isolated islands together. This work would form the basis for much of my work for the next six years, from 1964 through 1970.

The Nike missile family used very high performance chip-and-wire integrated circuits. It was decided to implement such a logic gate in Isolithic or AIM form. Bob McDonald and I laid out the necessary devices, had the masks made, and I processed the device through the model shop. For this early circuit, I used large (0.004 inch) inter-device spacings and ordinary isotropic (same rate in every direction) etching because advanced slot-forming techniques were not yet developed.

M. (Mike) Tomsky

To be more definite, after we drew the devices to scale, the mask shop made master drawings at 1000 times final size. The masters were checked for completeness and overlay or layer-to-layer alignment, and then photographically reduced to final size. The final photo emulsion-covered glass blanks, called masks, contained an x-y array of several hundred such circuits. Next, I wrote a flow sheet listing the steps needed to fabricate the device, obtained the starting material, and took masks, flow sheet, and starting material to the model shop. The model shop people performed most of the actual operations, with me looking over their shoulder where I thought necessary. Mike Tomsky, a lead man in the model shop liked my hands-on approach, and decided to take me under his wing, giving me guidance as what not to do with the shop people and so on.

We had also laid out the necessary metallization pattern on ceramic substrates for eventual mounting of the finished devices for test.

Highly magnified photographs of the first AIM devices are shown on the next two pages. The first page shows the circuits from the device side, while the second page shows the slot side. The magnification of the photographs is about 140X.

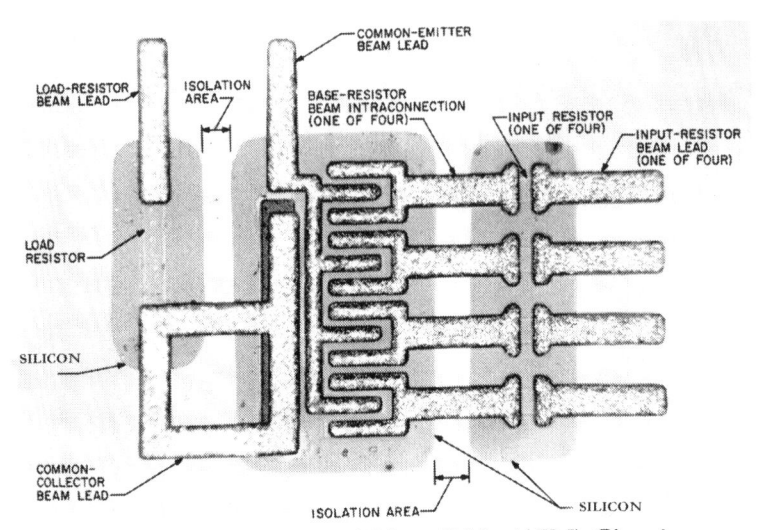

The First Air Isolated Monolithic (AIM) Circuit
Viewed face side up - details indicated on photo.

The first Air Isolated Monolithic (AIM) Circuit bonded to a metallized substrate. This is a four transistor logic gate. The load resistor is in the right bar of silicon, four transistors in the center, and the four input resistors in the left hand bar

Following the steps outlined in the preceding discussion, the completed devices were mounted on the substrates as shown above, and connected to external circuitry for testing. As expected, their performance was identical to that of the chip and wire circuits in all respects! We were all

113

ecstatic! The portion of the work performed on a military case was written up, and an abstract prepared for presentation at the 1964 IEDM.

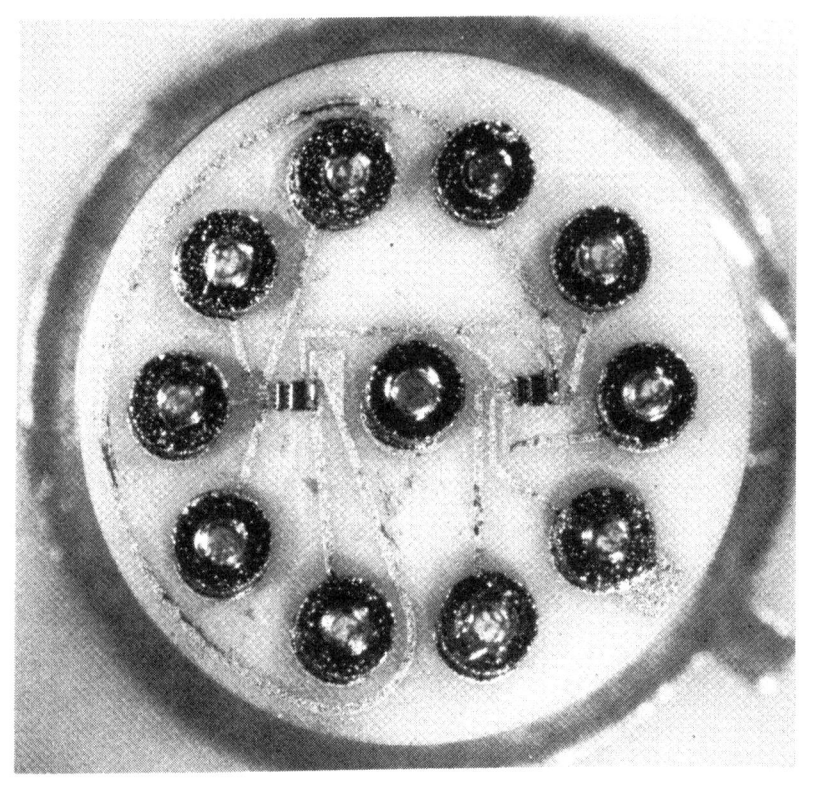

Two AIM 4-input gates mounted on a ceramic for testing.

As was usual procedure, the talk was not only approved for content, it was reviewed for style and presentation, including anticipated post-presentation questioning from the audience. The intent was to insure a favorable Bell Labs presentation, and many interested parties were present, including R. Ryder, and Eric Iwersen, and Jim

Nelson, Marty's supervisor. Finally we were ready for the presentation at the December 1964 IEEE International Electron Device Meeting in Washington DC. This was the most prestigious meeting of its kind in the world.

We were all in Washington, staying at the Washington Hilton, by now a familiar place. By this time, I was feeing pretty good about myself. While we were walking to eat, Marty was apparently nervous. When I contradicted a comment by Marty and made an incorrect statement about the expansion coefficients of polycrystalline silicon and bulk silicon, Marty exploded, venting his nervousness! He said something like, "That is the stupidest statement I have ever heard! If you do that again, I will beat the living SH*T out of you!" I was to learn that Marty had a photographic memory for what he had read, and could recite voluminous references verbatim. He was almost never wrong concerning little known or otherwise obscure facts.

Beam Leads Go Public at the IEDM – Dec 1964

Marty delivered the beam lead paper at the International Electron Device Meeting (IEDM) in Washington D C in the fall of 1964. Lepselter, Waggener, MacDonald, and Davis were coauthors. The talk was well received, and represented a turning point for the Bell System semiconductor effort. Marty had received recognition for his work, and was sitting on cloud nine. We continued to work together and became close friends. The beam lead approach eventually allowed Jack Morton to gracefully reverse his ground with respect to integrated circuits, but it would be awhile before that happened, and his influence faded away.

After the successful fabrication of the air-isolated circuits, Eric Iwersen assigned me the task of finding more precise means for exposing the beams, and for making isolation slots in Isoliths. The early silicon etches, mixtures of hydrofluoric and nitric acid, were isotropic, meaning that etching proceeded equally in both lateral and vertical directions. Thus, early designs had to have device (junction) edges far apart to enable high yield separation, thus greatly increasing overall device size, and reducing the economic advantage. These first circuits used 0.004 in junction-to-junction spacings and so were not very compact. I was to try to improve the situation by devising alternatives to permit closer junction spacings. The first try used a very fine form of sand blasting, which would turn out to be essentially a waste of time.

Sand Blasting and Light Activated Etching (cough, sneeze, or run away)

I first looked at sandblasting with "micron"-sized particles as a means for making slots. An SS White™

sandblasting station was purchased, and installed in a corner of my room. Special exhaust filters were added to the system, because we would be using extremely fine particles of silica and garnet in high-speed air streams to remove silicon under the beams and in the slots. Many combinations of particle size, particle material, and gas flow were tried. Control was poor and results were unsatisfactory. The small particles did not adequately differentiate between silicon and the beams. Without extreme care, the beams would either be mangled or entirely gone as a result of the separation process. Not only that, whenever I ran my super sandblaster, I would have hot flashes and acute breathing attacks, because I "knew" that the air was filled with enormous numbers of tiny particles that the filters could not remove. I knew of the plight of coal miners, and I readily imagined silicosis or worse. I gladly gave the sandblaster to one of the machine shops, and we were both happier. Yet another thing not to do!

I next looked at light activated etching, where chemical etching might proceed only where bright light impinged vertically directly on the silicon. Joe Ligenza was a physical chemist of considerable experience and ability, and when I asked him about the prospects he told me about the inter halogen compounds. There had been sporadic reports that compounds of chemicals, like iodine pentaflouride, that might display such properties, and it so happened that he had a lecture bottle of such a material. Such compounds are extremely toxic and corrosive, but when I asked Joe about how to store them, he said, "These things are so reactive, that they tend to react directly with moisture in the air. Only a big leak might be dangerous. Keep them in the bottom of your fume hood."

J. (Joe) Ligenza

I drew up and had built a small vacuum chamber for the experiments, and installed the entire apparatus in my very well exhausted fume hood that I had installed in my lab. I borrowed some high power mercury vapor lamps from coworkers and proceeded to experiment. The work was interesting and exciting, but not successful. I could remove silicon, but etching proceeded in all directions, and generally resulted in noxious materials being deposited on the wafer surfaces and the interior of the vacuum chamber that were difficult to remove, and to my mind, likely quite toxic. I bought and stored other fluorine bearing compounds other than iodine pentaflouride, under my fume hood, but none of them worked any better. Care and maintenance of the apparatus was a small nightmare. The most obvious result of my efforts was a series of nonfunctional mechanical vacuum pumps. The vacuum pumps contained organic oil that tended to polymerize, or form sludge/gunk, when exposed to the fluorine-bearing compounds. The pumps would freeze up when turned off after only a few runs. I was happy when this work was finished, even if it was a total failure. I had learned yet more things not to do.

A First Try at Anisotropic Etching

The third approach was based on a previously known anisotropic silicon etchant. Finne and Klien, just down the hall at Bell Labs, had developed a novel etching system for silicon based on pyrocatechol, ethylenediamine, and water. This system etched silicon at different rates in different directions in the silicon crystal. Thus, if the orientation of the silicon wafer was properly chosen, very well defined slots might be formed. The standard wafer orientation[7] was denoted by (111), pronounced "one, one, one".

---

[7] The use of the (111) orientation was a remnant of the earlier alloyed junction transistor technology. The dense (111) planes tended to keep the alloy junctions flat.

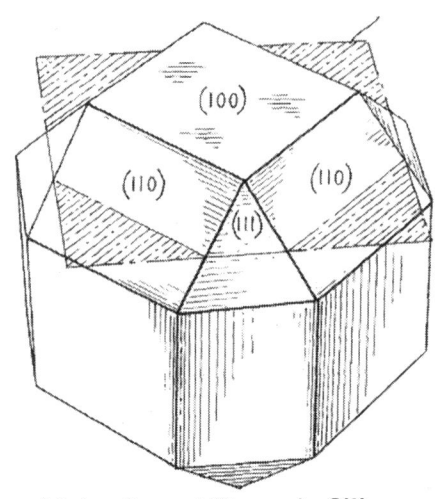

Major Crystal Planes in Silicon
The (111) direction etchs very slowly,
and the (100) direction etches rapidly
in hot alkaline solutions.

Since the etch rate in the (111) direction was essentially zero, the standard orientation was unsuitable for my purpose. The (100) direction[8] was the fastest etching direction, so in order to get the proper slot geometry; the (100) wafer orientation was needed. There was little evidence that (100) oriented silicon would yield devices significantly different from the prevalent (111) orientation, so I ordered (100) ingots, had them sliced and polished, and began to do etching experiments and fabricate devices. In the future it would turn out that there were indeed very significant differences in processing that would really retard rapid

---

[8] The symbols (100) and (110) are pronounced, "one, oh, oh" and "one, one, oh", respectively.

progress, but I would not know about these problems for several years in the future. In the meantime, I needed a material to serve as an etch mask.

Photoresist was not a suitable etch mask, since the available resists failed immediately in this solution. I obtained a Veeco™ vacuum system and electron beam deposition apparatus for depositing etching masks needed to use the crystallographic etches. I chose to evaporate silicon dioxide as an etching mask for these etches for two reasons. First, silicon dioxide dissolves very, very slowly in these etchants, and also because silicon dioxide is transparent in the infrared, so that front-back alignment is easy. In addition to the deposition conditions, procedures had to be developed for adequately cleaning the wafers prior to film deposition, because if the etch mask adhesion was poor, the etchants could attack under the mask causing uncertainty in the slot edge. Eventually I worked out these critical details and the mask formation process became routine.

I needed to know how to design the masks that were to result in isolation slots, so I performed a great many trial etches using candidate geometries, and was able to settle on a workable combination. Thus, I was able to specify the mask design rules for the major slots, while the situation at mask corners was still in flux.

Eric Iwersen and B. T. Murphy had designed a circuit incorporating novel features and I fabricated the devices in a manner similar to the earliest Isolithic circuits, but now I had reduced the device spacings to take advantage of the improved slot-making techniques that I had been developing. Iwersen, Murphy, and I had committed to a paper at the February 1965 IEEE ISSCC (International Solid State Circuit Conference) meeting in Philadelphia Pennsylvania, the most prestigious circuit design meeting in the world at that time.

The pyrocatechol anisotropic etchant refused to etch! The failure of the etching process threatened a disaster, because the reputations of the presenters would be at stake. Both Murphy and Iwersen were well known in the industry, but we would all suffer if the work were to be a failure. As the final hours approached, I had no alternative but to resort once more to isotropic etching to accomplish the device separation. A photograph from the press release describing the new circuit is shown on the next page.

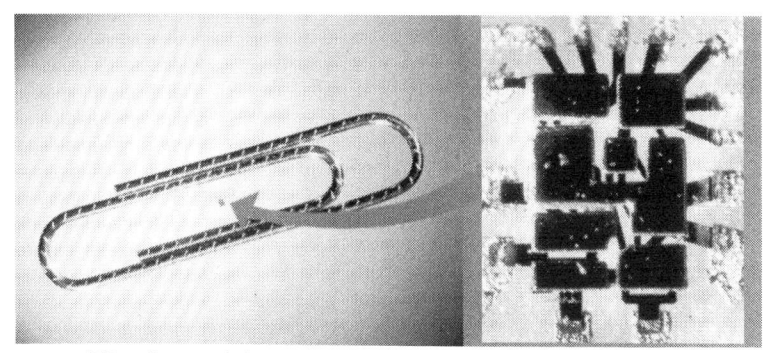

The Second Air Isolated Monolithic (AIM) Circuit
bonded to a metallized substrate for use. This is
a Murphy-Iwersen logic gate with hysteresis.

Fortunately, <u>isotropic</u> etching saved the day. I thinned the silicon on these devices to around one thousandth of an inch, half the value we wanted. The thinner silicon was necessary to successfully etch them apart using isotropic etching. The devices were so thin they were transparent to visible light. Under an ordinary microscope, the metallization was clearly visible through the silicon, even though it is not evident in the picture above. Working devices were obtained and measurements made that confirmed the predicted performance.

Eventually I abandoned this early anisotropic etching system. I did not yet understand why the etchant behaved so erratically. This understanding would not come until I invented electrochemically controlled thinning of silicon in 1969. It was to turn out that the beam lead metallization and silicon formed a battery, and the battery potential was forcing the silicon surface into a **passive** state.

An additional breakthrough in beam lead technology occurred in Allentown. Van Gelder and coworkers learned how to apply a contaminant-impervious layer of silicon nitride underneath the metallization prior to contact formation. This impervious layer located under the beam leads formed a barrier against all contaminants from the device surfaces, and when suitably formed, neatly solved another major cause of device failure, sodium contamination. The combination was called **Beam Lead Sealed Junction Technology.** It would eventually turn out that in some structures, there still existed a mechanism for sodium contamination, but this was not discovered for a few years. My contribution to the solution of this contamination problem would eventually save my bacon near the end of the Phase 2 project, and is discussed later on.

On 19 January 1965, the month before the ISSCC meeting, I **actually** wrote a summary of my third rotational assignment describing the use of the anisotropic etchant devised by Finne and Klein. I stayed in Iwersen's department until July 1966. I continued to work on devising better anisotropic etches to fabricate devices using the AIM approach.

In May of 1965, Eric Iwersen sent me to a University of Michigan intensive two-week course, "Semiconductor Theory and Technology", a cram course relevant to my current field of endeavor. Eric had made a good decision. The course enabled me to rapidly get an overview of semiconductors that I would have been unable to easily gain when immersed in the details of my job. When I returned to Murray Hill, I plunged into my assigned task: making a denser, more robust Air Isolation technique.

The University of Michigan
Engineering Summer Conferences

This certifies that Herbert A. Waggener has satisfactorily completed the special summer course in Semiconductor Theory & Technology

Date May 28 1965

Dean, College of Engineering
Professor in Charge

End-Marked AIM pnpn arrays with Air Crossovers and Fuses

A group in Holmdel represented by M. F. Slana, was interested in the possibility of using arrays of four layer devices to make electronic switching networks where switch closure and maintenance was controlled largely by network organization and the inherent properties of the devices themselves. I laid out an array of such devices and incorporated an additional feature in the design envisioned by Lepselter, air crossovers. The use of these crossovers also permitted the formation of a reliable fuse, whereby defective devices could be reliably and selectively removed from the array even when it was in service, if desired. M. F. Slana and I filed for a patent, "Switching Network" on 2 May 1967. Patent # 3,504,131, "Switching Network" was issued on 31 March 1970. I have no record of either internal or external technical reports that may have been generated.

The Alkali Metal Hydroxide / Alcohol Etchants - 1966

I began a systematic investigation of mixtures of the alkali metal and organic hydroxides in water, and found that they too were highly anisotropic as was the Finne-Klein system, but with superior reproducibility and without questionable organic compounds. Like the pyrocatechol mix, all of these etches exhibited very low etch rates in the (111) direction, high etch rates in the (100) direction and various etch rates in the (110), or corner, direction. I looked at lithium, sodium, rubidium, and cesium hydroxides as well as tetra-methyl and related ammonium hydroxides. I eventually settled on potassium hydroxide as the alkaline ingredient. I found that if the corner etching rates were too low, pyramidal defects would form, where the silicon stopped etching locally, thereby causing inter-island shorts, ruining the isolation. It was as if there was some sort of tiny invisible mask that somehow caused the local corner etch rate to be <u>very</u> small, but I could never find the underlying source of the problem. I had to resort to arranging for the corner etch rate to be large enough to allow these local masks to be undermined, as envisioned by R. Kragness.

I found that the (110) etch rate could be influenced by adding simple alcohols. By adding n-propanol, I could get a moderate etch rate. Unfortunately, this corner etch rate depended upon how much silicon was dissolved in the etchant. The introduction of sec-butanol had the opposite effect. Sec-butanol suppressed corner etching, and had an opposite effect with regard the amount of dissolved silicon. Happily, the combination of n-propanol and sec-butanol provided a good balance. This dual alcohol composition exhibited a moderate amount of corner attack, and relative insensitivity to the effects of silicon content. I had at least one useful etchant. Roger Kragness, a coworker and fellow CDT graduate, was involved with evaluating my etch compositions.

A joint patent application for the KOH / n-propanol / sec butyl alcohol etches, was filed on Dec 20, 1966, 1 November 1967 and patent #3,506,509 was finally issued on

14 April 1970. This patent was to be replaced by another, 3,765,969 to be filed 13 July 1970, and issued 16 October 1973.

One further major problem remained. The alkali hydroxide/alcohol etchants had an amazing ability to attack or remove the material used to mount the wafer to the sapphire disc used for thinning, thereby ruining everything. Miscellaneous debris in the bottom of the etching container is hardly useful. A. L. Tyler, a polymer chemist from the Allentown works was to be later brought in to work on the problem and found a formulation that was suitable. This material and technique was patented with A. L. Tyler as inventor.

We Buy a House Foundation in NJ (Apr 66) and are Transferred to Allentown Pennsylvania (Jul 66)

The move to Walton Avenue had paid off. The combined effect of the savings in house payments and an annual salary of $14,303.94 (two salary raises) had enabling us to generate some savings. We had found a small two-story colonial in a Morris Plains subdivision, well within driving range of Murray Hill. On 12 April 1966, we cashed in some of our AT&T stock, ponied up some savings, deposited $2,940, and signed a contract with the developer. We looked forward to being homeowners, acquiring equity and stability for a change, instead of throwing rent money down a rat hole.

New Years Party at the Lannings - 1966
L to R: Mr Dick's Hand, Dorothy Dick,
Ron & Maxene Holmes,
Marge & Earl Lanning, and Wife Judy Waggener

The house construction had gotten to the point where the foundation was poured when I received word that I was being transferred to Allentown. My first reaction was shock and dismay! I had failed in my attempt to be competitive within the Murray Hill technical universe. I was now to be forever doomed by being discarded to the second tier. I was to be banished to Allentown, home of the ordinary.

There were considerable differences between the technical staffs of Murray Hill and Allentown. The Murray Hillians were generally self confident to the point of arrogance, and the Allentownians were more guarded and defensive, especially when in the presence of their intellectual

129

rivals from the Hill. Many of the Allentown Bell Guys in turn looked down on the Western Electric Manufacturing Engineers, in a completely similar fashion.

People at Murray Hill were paid more, were generally more prestigious, and were more highly ranked than their Allentown counterparts. All this seemed quite natural to me when I was at Murray Hill, as I looked down upon the lesser ability of the poor Allentown beggars.

Now **I** was to be an Allentown person, not by an accident of hiring, but by evolutionary winnowing forces! What a prospect! I really had some soul searching to do. It was true that Jim Early had recently become Director of the Allentown Bell Labs, and it was true that Roger Kragness had been transferred before me. Jim Early assured me that I would not only fit in, I would enrich the staff. To me, this sounded quite similar to the comments made when someone was asked to leave the company.

On the plus side, the transfer made a lot of sense, even though I hated the thought. There was a demand for high performance bipolar integrated circuits, and AIM technology had the potential to meet that need. There was no one who was in a better position to put AIM into production than I was, and I knew it. Balancing my despair against the needs of the company, I reluctantly accepted the transfer.

There was another small problem besides my bent psyche. We had just plunked down our hard-saved money, and were now the proud owners of a foundation in Morris Plains, so we were not in a position to make a down payment on a house near Allentown. The Corporate Executive Instructions provided no guidance regarding this eventuality, so for some time we were in financial never-never land. What was worse, mortgage rates in Pennsylvania were escalating to stratospheric levels. By the time the down payment money was returned to us, **no mortgage loans** were available in Pennsylvania! The state usury law mandating an interest cap of 22 percent had been reached, and money dried up, to Zero!

Judy and I were stuck. We had clawed our way to home ownership in Morris Plains, and now the transfer and circumstance had snatched it away. We moved into 814 S. Hays Street, a rental property on the southeastern edge of Allentown, where we needed no down payment. When my new home department found out about the hole in the Chief Executive Instructions, They allowed me to voucher the amount to pay for our foundation contract out of departmental funds. It would be nearly a year until a combination of salary, interest rates, personal loans, and creative pricing by the builder allowed us to buy a new home.

131

I had often had lively conversations regarding the shortcomings of our local Bell management with Eric, and I would often comment that my dissatisfaction was similar to a tempest in a teapot. As was customary, I was given a going away party to "celebrate" my transfer. I recall little of the party, except that Eric gave me an inlaid teapot with a poem taped to it. The poem began:

| Look to thy loins O Allentown |
| Tag Waggener is coming down. |
| He'll give you all but little peace |
| And call thy Supervisors geese! |

The original poem was much longer, but the paper was lost long, long ago. Only the teapot remains in my possession.

Eric Iwersen's Teapot for my Tempests.

I also received a pair of Telephone Pole climbing leg spikes, just in case I would need to get another job, or aspire to become head of AT&T. I still have the Pole Climbers in 2010, and there were times when I thought that I should learn how to use them.

Sister Suzanne and husband Tom Mower were living in Kansas City Missouri, where they had two children, Douglas John, was born in April of 1965, and Melissa Nan, was born in June of 1966. In the near future, we would be able to see them when we returned to the Midwest for our annual visits, but the reverie would not last. Douglas was to die in March of 1967, while the family lived in Lake Quivera Kansas, a short distance from Kansas City.

Chapter 4 – The Allentown Experience - July 1966

In Allentown, my supervisor was Mitch Stickler, who reported to John Forster, who in turn reported to Jim Early. Mitch was a hard working intelligent guy, who had been given the job of running the Bell Labs Process Development Lab (PDL). The PDL had a full complement of around 14 unionized Western Electric operators, a section chief, several Bell Labs MTS, and other technical staff in charge of the technical aspects of the facility. Mitch had little interest in semiconductor processing, and wanted to concentrate on software problems. **Mitch thus turned the facility operation over to me lock, stock, and barrel**! The facility had been in existence for a while and I was to find that it had developed a character of it's own. That is, it firmly reflected the interest and intent of the imbedded staff.

When the PDL was turned over to me, I first familiarized myself with the personnel and the specific processes available. Except for beam leads and the nascent AIM technology, the <u>detailed</u> operational aspects of the rest of the steps were unfamiliar to me. I knew the names and functions of each step in a textbook sense, and how to put them in the proper order to fabricate devices, but the complex chemistry, physics, and mechanics behind most steps were unknown to me, or to anyone else not intimately involved. The existing recipes had been developed over time and were largely a matter of history. Any success was largely dependent upon the actions of all forebears having done their jobs properly in the first place. I was to find out that the assumption of proper prior process development was only partly valid.

I found that when I wanted to dig into the details of a particular operation, the operation was generally carried out according to written instructions, but with personal interpretations that depended upon the particular operator, modified by the applicable technical overseer. Most steps were essentially copies of similar steps at Murray Hill, and in our Reading PA plant. The situation was pretty easy to understand and to steer, except for **Photolithography**.

Photolithography was the outstanding exception, and a real problem area. I was to find that the actual detailed steps were in constant flux, changing in detail from moment-to moment. The lithography lead man and the lithographic "engineer" zealously guarded the details of the lithography steps from outside eyes. It was as though lithography was influenced or directed by some mystical factors, and only the highest of priests were privy to the inner workings. Other than the general overall lithographic steps, I found it impossible to gain detailed information or control of this operation. I would have had to either fire these guys or transfer them elsewhere to gain control, and they knew it. They were confident that they could simply wait me out, and were also certain that they were some of the best photolithographers in the business. I would learn that this overconfidence was epidemic in self-proclaimed lithography experts. The "transcendent lithographer" phenomenon would continue to reappear in several different instances later in my career.

I had two main tasks to perform: Develop production-worthy AIM technology, and install beam leads in the PDL. I had neither the charter nor energy to revamp the lithography or really shake down the entire facility. My failure to revamp lithography and other entrenched practices were mistakes that I would pay for in times to come. In the future, I would not make such a mistake again. In the meantime, I set about introduction of beam leads and AIM technologies, my areas of expertise.

I ordered, assembled, tested, and characterized an electron beam deposition station to deposit silicon dioxide for making the AIM etching mask. I also set up the AIM etching station, along with the associated cleaning steps. I then set up the vacuum deposition forward/back sputtering system for performing all the necessary metallization steps for beam leads. After writing up instructions, I turned it all over to operators for routine operation. I then turned to further refinement of the AIM separation process.

Roger Kragness had earlier suggested that extra features could be added to the exterior corners of the etch-apart mask to permit use of etchants with greater corner undercutting. These added features would simply be etched away just as the etching was finished, thereby leaving only beautifully pristine slots. As a major benefit, larger corner etch rates essentially eliminated residual pyramidal defects as a yield phenomenon. Only an adequate mounting material needed to be developed in order to enable sustained high yield AIM circuit fabrication.

A. L. Tyler, a polymer chemist from a sister department, was assigned the task of finding a mounting material for AIM slices that would resist the anisotropic etchant. He found a mixture of two polymers, butadiene and styrene, that would work satisfactorily. This material could be placed between the wafer and sapphire disc, the wafer forced into contact against the disc, and then cured in place. A remaining problem was how to remove the hardened stuff after the slots were formed and separated devices tested. At Lamont's suggestion, we found that high concentrations (3%) of highly toxic ozone gas in oxygen would cause the material to slowly and gracefully vaporize, leaving the finished devices ready to pick up for wet cleaning and final assembly. We finally had **all** the main pieces, including the nitride junction seal, in place to begin routine processing of AIM devices.

Ready, Set, Process AIM Devices

A primary purpose of the PDL was to fabricate exploratory chips designed by device people at Allentown and other areas. We began processing two types of devices. The logic devices designed by R. Pederson and others at Allentown, and arrays of phototransistors designed by Sam Broydo at Murray Hill.

Most of the devices fabricated were digital logic circuits or chips. Several of these chips were designed for people in the Indian Hill BTL facility in Naperville Illinois. Indian hill was designing a new generation of switching system and had placed severe performance demands on the logic to be employed. In their opinion, standard integrated circuit technology was simply too slow so the very high performance AIM technology was required to meet to meet the system needs. On the other hand, they had no experience in designing systems operating at such speeds, and in addition, this fast AIM technology was new, with unproven reliability. They decided to build a large mockup that essentially ran set programs repeatedly, so that the error and failure rate could be measured. We supplied the hundreds to thousands of chips needed for the test, and waited for the test to be completed some time in the future. The device yields were not spectacular, but fabricating the required number of parts was not a problem.

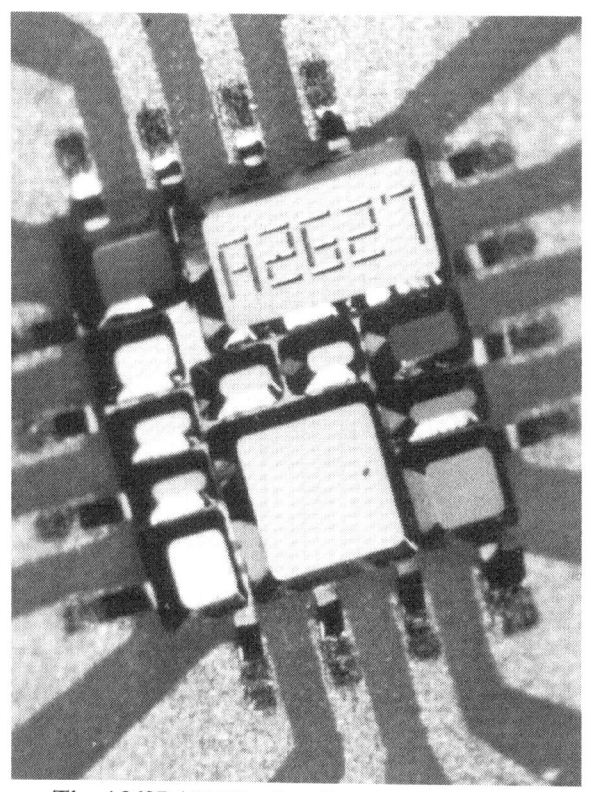

The A2627 AIM Device, Bonded to Substrate
Bell Labs Record, Oct/Nov 1966 p 316

Both my facility in Allentown and a group located at our Reading PA plant also fabricated AIM devices. The Reading devices were intended for undersea cable applications. Their circuits operated at all-time record propagation delay speeds of around 700 picoseconds! In contrast, the first Nike AIM devices clocked in at around 4000

141

picoseconds, with similar device technology! **The designers and system customers were ecstatic.**

We Buy a House in Allentown – 1967

We were living in the rented house on Hays street in the southwest corner of Allentown waiting for the interest rate problem to resolve itself, which it soon did. Interest rates were high (>20%), but at least mortgage loans again became available. Because of the high interest rates, we were priced out of many homes we would have liked. I simply didn't make enough to qualify, an age-old problem. We were able to arrange a deal with a local builder whereby he inflated the initial cost of the house enough that with only a small personal loan from George Richards[9] to add to our next egg, we were able to qualify for the minimum 20 percent down payment. On 19 October 1966, we contracted for a house to be built by a well-known local builder. The building lot was only one and a half blocks from our rental and within a few months we were the proud owners of a small two-story colonial house located at 713 South Ott St, a few blocks south of Muhlenberg Lake, part of a really nice park in the west end of Allentown. Our first mortgage payment was made on 2/3/67, so I think that we moved there in January.

---

[9] George Richards was a chess-playing BTL friend in Murray Hill, NJ.

We moved into the house with no particular difficulty, except that there was no lawn and mud was a constant enemy. The mud would remain until we were able to grow a lawn in the spring. On the other hand, we felt that the ground would probably be frozen for a while. We were wrong.

Shawn & her Bike, 713 S. Ott, Allentown PA - Spring 1967
Note the state of the Lawn. Mud, Mud, Mud!

Also on the negative side was the complete absence of trees. We had been promised four trees, but when they arrived in the spring, the four "trees" were ten-foot long bare-root sticks. The spindly sticks were quickly placed in shallow holes dug by the nurseryman. The nurseryman disappeared just as quickly as he had come. It was annoying when our sticks would fall over in a gentle breeze. I had to replant

143

them, and attach guy wires to keep them in place. Despite the sad appearance of the bare root spindly sticks, in the spring sunshine, limbs and leaves soon began to grow. The trees would be quite handsome by the time we left in 1973, five years in the future. Eventually the grass grew, the mud disappeared, and we landscaped the lot. The house was at the bottom end of a long gentle hill, and so was in a position to collect runoff. Fortunately, the builder had only half submerged the basement, and we had a very dry house no matter how hard the rain.

Photo Session Gone a bit Awry at 713 S. Ott

We planted (and repositioned several times) a willow tree in the back of our yard that really liked the runoff water. The linemen from the utility company were not so enamored with our tree. Judy wanted to plant a clump of birch trees in the front yard, and we did so. While we were working in the front yard early one evening, Mark asked, "Why is the Moon Green"? When we looked up, not only was the moon the wrong color, it was way too big, and growing larger. It would turn out that what we were seeing was the result of a satellite launched from Wallops Island Virginia. They were examining the effects of alkali metal dispersal in the stratosphere. The sunlight reflecting off the expanding ball of alkali ions was certainly attention getting while it lasted!

Our family and Others at Muhlenberg Lake, Allentown PA- 1967+

Once again this summer our vacation trip to the Midwest would be taken in July. As usual, we divided our time between our parents, first visiting Des Moines Iowa and later on, going south to Lakeside Missouri. The families of both Suzanne and Buddy had arranged to be there as well. It was great to see everyone, but these visits were just too short before we would have to return to the Labs. In later years we would move to Skokie Illinois, so the logistics for visiting family were much improved, but that move would not occur until 1973, when I transferred to the Teletype Corporation.

The Waggeners at Lakeside Missouri – July 1967.
Seated, L to R: Mom, Wade, Mark, Melissa, Carol, and Chris.
Standing, L to R: Katharine, Herb, Shawn, Suzanne, Tom, John, Judy, and Buddy. Dad took the Picture.

We Go to Press, and Publicly Disclose the AIM Technology

On 1 Nov 1967, the patent application "Etchant for Precision Etching of Semiconductors", by Kragness and Waggener, had been filed. I presented the paper. "Anisotropic Etching for Forming Isolation Slots in Silicon Beam Leaded Integrated Circuits', H. A. Waggener, R. C. Kragness and A. L. Tyler at the December 1967 IEDM meeting in Washington DC.

146

The announcement received some attention. Following the talk, a press release was held, and an information package released to the press in anticipation of a favorable response. I was featured on the cover of the December 1967 Solid State Technology magazine, and a short note was printed on page 73 of the magazine (overleaf).

SST Front Cover Showing HAW depositing SiO2 for
Air Isolation Mask formation - Dec 1967

147

An improved etching technique permits more efficient fabrication of integrated circuits. These drawings show the advantage of using a new preferential etchant in making integrated circuits. Active regions (the p-type silicon) of a circuit can be spaced closer together when the new etching technique is used. This means more devices can be made on each slice. Completed devices on a slice are etched apart from the back, i.e., with the diffused face of the slice down as shown. Other chemical etchants etch sideways as fast as downward, making precise control of the width of the slot impossible (left). The new etchant developed at Bell Telephone Laboratories etches preferentially; that is, a wedge-shaped slot with a flat bottom is formed that narrows as etching progresses (right). Two of the primary lattice planes of silicon are labeled with the conventional Miller indices. The class of preferential etchants now being investigated at Bell Laboratories consists of strongly basic, or alkaline, solutions. One such etchant, formulated for silicon, is comprised of potassium hydroxide, propanol, and water. The masking operation is done after the desired devices have been fabricated on one side of the slice. A silicon dioxide mask is applied to the opposite side. This mask delineates the slots for etching. Because the sides of the slots are stationary, only relatively simple etching controls are required. The etching technique is described in a paper by H. A. Waggener, R. C. Kragness, and A. L. Tyler of Bell Telephone Laboratories and presented recently at the International Electron Devices Meeting.

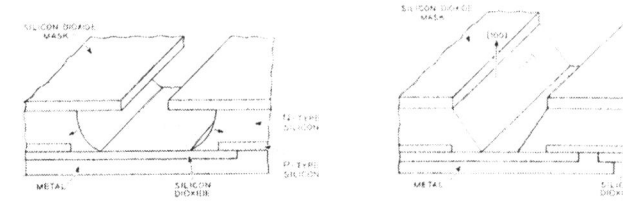

Solid State Technology note on p73 - Dec 1967

Sam Broydo Analyzes Photo Transistor Arrays –1968

The optical arrays being processed for Sam Broydo at Murray Hill represented another aspect of our effort. These phototransistor arrays were to be used as detectors in an exploratory optical memory system using holographic storage techniques. Barry Soloway was the Allentown designer who was processing phototransistor arrays for Sam.

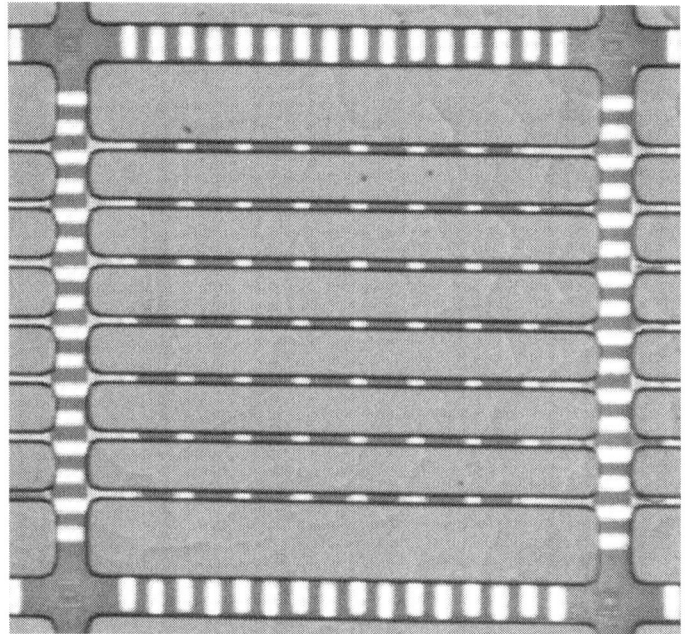

Photodetector Arrays Designed by S. Broydo
Processed at Allentown, after separation etching, but before testing.

My PDL was making arrays for the experimental optical memory system Sam was working on in Murray Hill. The yield of these arrays was very poor. Sam was a brilliant analyst, and began characterizing the arrays we had made to deduce failure modes. According to Sam, one day when I met him in the hall, I said, "I understand that you are having some problems. If you need any help, come see me". He did, and we began to form a bond of mutual interest.

Sam found that AIM devices had multiple problems, to put it mildly. The first problem he found was related to the photolithographic mask manufacturing techniques. The mask shop simply could not make masks with the required precision. The array yields would inevitably be limited by mask generation technology, at least for the design rules he was using.

More importantly for me, Sam also found three other problems, which were directly related to the AIM technology itself. First, he deduced that the PDL standard processing resulted in device base regions with unusually low surface doping profiles. These doping profiles resulted in excess emitter-collector leakage currents due inversion of the base region. These doping profiles turned out to be due to unexpected but very significant processing differences in the way that (100) and (111) oriented silicon oxidize. These processing differences would have to be addressed, if success was to be achieved.

Equally troubling, he found that on many chips, regions of silicon nitride were peeling off the surface. It was already well known that the deposited nitride layer was under severe tension, and that under the right conditions, a nitride crack could begin at a slot edge, and sometimes result in a small region of the nitride popping completely off the die, resulting in what I called a "manhole cover"! The local absence of the nitride junction seal then made the chip vulnerable to alkali contamination, thereby ruining the reliability of that device.

Sam also identified two additional device failures associated with the AIM process itself; bubbles or voids in the mounting material, and physical cracks in the silicon that had been created in the course of the mounting and/or the thinning process. Sam detected mask and lithographic problems as well, but these problems were not due to the AIM or beam lead steps, but were at least partially due to my self-proclaimed lithographic gurus.

The work of Sam was invaluable. By identifying these problems, the work enabled modifications to the starting sequence to improve the overall process. That was one of the fundamental reasons for having a facility like the PDL. It might be painful, but better to find out this kind of problem at a low volume pilot level rather than when running full tilt.

My Final Year Working at Allentown –1968

We continued to process devices throughout 1968. The process sequences continued to be honed and improved, but the situation was relatively featureless. While in charge of the PDL, in late 1967, I identified another yield limiting step associated with the initial deposition and etching of the beam lead technology itself. I discovered that the self-indicating silicide contact window step could still result in open circuited devices, and figured out how to minimize the problem. I issued a Technical Memorandum on the subject on 9 Jan 1968 titled "Excessive Contact Resistance in Beam Lead Devices". It was not clear if anyone was paying attention.

We were continuing to remove yield killers from the AIM process. Depositing somewhat thinner nitride layers eliminated the nitride cracking and manhole cover problem. The formation of voids in the mounting medium was solved by first allowing a droplet of mounting material to flow slowly over the entire wafer surface, and only then placing the sapphire mounting disc so as to allow bubble-free spreading between substrate and wafer. Following this complete spreading of fluid, the excess could now be squeezed out to result in intimate contact without voids or gaps. Cracking of the silicon during mechanical thinning was eliminated by curing the mounting material to a softer more elastic consistency, and by using precision surface grinding[10] for initial wafer thinning instead of lapping. The technology was now maturing and exhibiting more consistently high yields. Unknown to me, the (100) silicon material responds

---

[10] We used a precision Blanchard™ Grinder with diamond grit - fast, accurate, and low damage.

differently than (111) to thermal processing and possibly cleaning steps. It differed in ways I would only fully realize at the Teletype Corporation facilities, in 1974 and later.

Meanwhile, the system tests in Indian Hill had proceeded without a single logical error, over more than a year's operation, and with the exception of the photo arrays, device yields had become stable and meeting our (perhaps limited) expectations.

Electroplating Control for Beam Leads – Another Masterpiece - 1968

When Marty invented beam leads, he envisioned that each of the two separate plating steps were to be accomplished in a very controlled manner, not too thin or too thick, just the right amount. Electroplating of gold is nearly ideal, in the sense that for almost every electron that passes into a plating cell, one gold atom is plated. Thus how much current flows into an object determines precisely how much gold is plated onto it For practical reasons, the total area being plated on a wafer was unknown, and a fixed voltage was applied to the cell. Since the area being plated was unknown, the resulting plating thickness had to be determined experimentally.

Marty used an electroplating technique called meniscus plating for his early models, and this technique was used in production. In meniscus plating, the wafer is held by the edges, and placed face down so as to just touch the plating solution containing a counter electrode, and then withdrawn slightly to form a meniscus, keeping the plating solution away from the back side of the wafer, and a fixed voltage is applied to the cell. In order to achieve tight control, periodic microscopic inspection was necessary, because different codes had different fractional areas to be plated. This inspection added significantly to the cost of the beam lead process.

I devised an electroplating approach that circumvented differences in plating thickness resulting from differences in plating area.

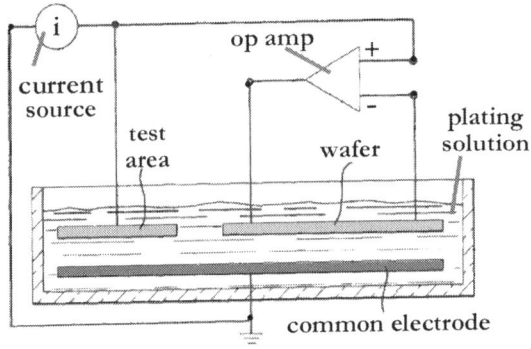

Drawing modified from Patent # 3,627,648

The control dial could be set to achieve the desired final thickness, and the final result would be independent of the open area to be plated, a significant simplification. In this technique, a <u>predetermined electric current</u> is passed through a <u>standard test area</u> immersed in the plating solution, and the resulting voltage is measured using an operational amplifier, or op amp. This measured voltage was then applied by the output of the op amp to the actual wafers to be plated. The bath geometry was made so that the physical condition of the test wafers was identical to the target wafers, so that the test area and target wafers were being plated at the same current density.

This arrangement insured constant current density regardless of exposed wafer area, and thus allowed unattended electroplating to any pre-specified thickness, without an intervening visual inspection. Only an inspection was needed to verify the final thickness. A patent for the plating technique was filed on 9 April 1969. Patent # 3,627,648, "Electroplating Method" was issued 14 December 1971. I don't know whether the technique was ever applied to the plating of beam leads on the production lines, but I was proud of the conception nonetheless.

Some Events Leading to a Very, Very Foolish Action

I had pushed hard while at Allentown to get air isolation into production, the task with which I had been charged. Some of the irritations were minor and should have been ignored. One such incident occurred as we were preparing for a system-wide Department Head show, in which the PDL and I had roles to play, as AIM was being presented as a major achievement of this Lab. The Sunday afternoon the day before the show, I needed to put my display material in front of the PDL. I parked in the otherwise empty Western Electric main parking lot to go to practice the presentation, about one quarter mile from the Western Electric Guarded entrance, since the Bell Lab entrance was closed. When I reached the entrance carrying the display material that I had worked on at home, the guard said, "Your car is pointed in the wrong direction, and you will have to go back and turn it around before you can enter the plant". I blinked and sputtered in disbelief, but did as directed.

When I returned from my car, I started to pick up the display material when he said; "You can't bring that material into the plant. It has not been authorized!" I was dumbfounded, fuming and was more than a little cross. I swore a little, and insisted on getting his name and badge number, explaining to him that I would let the watch commander and the plant manager know that this guard was personally responsible for ruining an important part of tomorrow's presentation. After the guard returned to normal color, he grudgingly let me take the material into the facility.

The next day, the presentation went well, but I was becoming disillusioned with the setup. When I later commented on the subject of the parking lot incident to Jim Early he said, "That sort of thing used to bother me, but now I simply use my key to let myself into the BTL entrance". That really helped me a lot. I had no magic key and had no way of avoiding either the idiots or their idiocy.

I pushed the envelope a little on another incident. I was working long hours because the PDL was working on two shifts, and one morning I decided to come to work with a straw "coolie" hat. I was met at the guard gate and not allowed to enter the facility with the hat. I protested, but to no avail, it was "against the Western Electric rules". Just to be obstinate, I repeated the act throughout the week, until I finally got tired of the game.

There was another type of situation that was much more troublesome. The PDL used many toxic liquid and gaseous materials, as did all semiconductor facilities of the time. The liquid toxic materials were enclosed in exhausted stations known as "Allentown Hoods", or in exhausted storage cabinets. The Allentown Hood had a particulate air filter on top and was exhausted at the front lip and rear edges. When the flows were correctly adjusted, filtered air entered the top and partly blew into the room and was partly captured by the exhausts at the front and rear edges, along with any toxic fumes. These hoods did not work as envisioned when the flow of filtered air was too high or the level of exhaust was too low. In such cases, toxic fumes could escape into the room.

Unfortunately, the fresh air and exhaust blowers were mounted in the attic, and were the responsibility of plant engineering. The two sets of blowers were independently powered, and there was no means to measure or monitor the momentary pressures or flow balance. The integrity of the hood exhaust system thus depended upon weather conditions!

On occasions when operators noticed fumes coming from the hoods, we would evacuate the area, and I would inform the plant department of the problem. Most often, I would be given a shrug, and a promise to look into it. Complaints to my management also fell on deaf ears, and the situation was not resolved. In one instance, Jim Early's Administrative Assistant ran to my door shouting, "Tag, there is acetone in the sewer system! We need to find the source! The whole building could blow up!" I told him something like; "Go to hell, an explosion will simply kill many people at once, instead of a few over a longer term. Go find it yourself!" There was neither an explosion, nor were the balancing controls installed while I worked there. The Administrative Assistant never asked me for my help again.

On one occasion, I was at home sound asleep when I got a call from the Western Electric Medical Department informing me that some of my workers were in the infirmary due to a gross failure of the exhaust system, and the resulting exposure to fumes.

I put on my clothes and arrived at the plant in around a half hour, this time parking in the correct direction in the parking lot. I first went to the facility, and examined the exhaust system where a motor had failed. I then headed down to the infirmary, told them who I was, and reported what I had found. The attending physician looked at me, my blood-shot eyes, and announced that this was a result of the fumes, and that I should be given oxygen immediately. I told him no, my eyes were red because I had been awakened from a sound sleep a few minutes ago, and was not yet up to speed. Further, I said that in no event would I accept oxygen. The exhaust system was repaired, the workers released, and I went back home to bed. The plant engineering and maintenance people had triumphed again. The above incidents challenged my patience and fed my desire to see some changes in management, and would eventually induce me to act very, very foolishly.

Somewhere around this time, John H. Forster was transferred elsewhere and Jim Bodfro[11] took his place. I was to find that where John had been supportive, Jim Bodfro was not. Not only was Bodfro non-supportive to me, he

---

[11] A pseudonym.

represented a branch of the Allentown BTL that seemed highly critical of anything that originated in Murray Hill. Jim was only one of several members of the Allentown staff that held this opinion. A number of us came to consider this particular band of Allentown Individuals cultural and technical cutthroats. It sometime seemed that they liked complaining about imposed problems rather than working on solutions and thereby earning their keep.

I was definitely not a member of their camp, nor did I want to be. I admit that I considered them a bit ineffectual and their behavior regressive. On several occasions, I would get reports that members of this loose Allentown Alliance had either suppressed data or outright lied about results in important meetings with higher management. To say that this wholesome group did little to support me would be an understatement.

Technological innovation in bipolar integrated circuit technology continued. A guy named Glinsky at Murray Hill invented a process called Collector Diffusion Isolation or CDI. This technology was much more space efficient than the earlier junction isolation techniques, which made these devices more cost effective than previously available in the standard isolation design, so the expected cost reduction afforded by AIM over CDI was reduced, but the AIM performance edge remained. There was little doubt in anyone's mind, including mine, that CDI was a viable technology. Not only was the CDI process cost effective, no new technology was needed in the factory to implement it. Circuit performance was not much changed over the older design, but there was a considerable cost improvement due to the higher circuit density.

My Most Foolish Action, Bad Boss Bashing – mid 1967 or early 1968

When a stable AIM process had been fashioned, I wanted to release AIM to production and move on to new challenges. Jim Early had sent an early heads-up letter to the Western Electric management, but failed to follow through. The release to production required Jim's signature, but he could not bring himself to release it. All the available yield and reliability data looked good, but he still sat on the release, as far as I could ascertain, just sitting woodenly. We discussed the problem a number of times but he was still comatose when asked for some action.

After vacillation lasting some months, Jim Early could still not bring himself to make a decision. One day in a fit of madness[12] I said something to him like, "You are truly incompetent as a manager! You have fretted about this release for months and still cannot make a decision! You should be fired! If your bosses don't know about your inability yet, they soon will, because I am going to tell them!" After I had spoken, I turned on my heel and walked out of his office, not knowing what the future would bring.

Nothing immediately obvious happened as a result of my outburst, but I had inflicted severe damage upon myself. The fact that I might have been correct did not change the fact that I had driven a spear into the belly of my glorious leader in a frontal attack. He decided to keep me on, but to treat me more like a technician than a star. He got even, and probably thought little more about the matter. I was not pilloried nor expelled; but my relative income began to fall even further.

As I said before, the people at Indian Hill, Bell Labs, Naperville had operated the test of their AIM devices for a year **without a single error**. Now these same people had discovered that a crucial mistake had been made in their choice of the circuit card connectors to be used in the new high speed switching system for which the high-speed AIM devices had been developed. To their astonishment and

---

[12] I eventually realized that my modern-day Don Quixote imitation was the stupidest thing I have ever done.

dismay, the chosen connector had a large inductance in the grounding arrangement that caused severe digital signal degradation in the system. The supposedly quiet digital grounds had noise that was **at least half of the designed signals**! Under these conditions, the system could not possibly work!

Obviously, the high-speed AIM devices were switching much faster than their chosen ground planes could accommodate. The design of the physical system had progressed so far that system delivery date would suffer if they were forced to redesign the hardware to get better grounding. They decided that the "best solution" was to substitute much lower speed devices, with the same logical functions, and change the system specifications! Thus, the higher speed of the AIM devices was transformed into an AIM killer. Perhaps this was the reason that Jim had been reluctant to put the devices into production.

This event was depressing, to say the least. I did my best to numb my mind and slog on, but it was a real problem.

I continued to work at Allentown for a while, but it soon became apparent to me that I was going nowhere. I had a cadre of supporters and continued to interact well with many of the Allentown people, but not with those in my direct management path. It was a miserable existence (for all).

I was well on my way to becoming a technician, and second rate at that.

Chapter 5 – My Return to Murray Hill and Redemption – 1969

To my astonishment and delight, I was offered the opportunity to return to Murray Hill. Marty Lepselter had previously been promoted to Department Head of the Exploratory Semiconductor Technology Department, reporting to David Thomas, who was now his Director.

Martin P. (Marty) Lepselter

Marty had an immediate problem that desperately needed a solution, and he thought that I might be able to help. He asked me if I was willing to return to Murray Hill. He had made inquiries as to whether my Allentown management was willing to release me, as in those days Human Resource functions were largely absent. Allentown reluctantly (?) agreed to release me, and I could hardly be restrained! As I recall, I was loaned out even before the formal transfer was finalized. I feel fairly sure that my Allentown management was not unhappy with my leaving. **In any case, up to that time, I was the only person who, once having been transferred to Allentown, was able to return to Murray Hill.** I returned to Murray Hill somewhat dented, but **Alive!**

I rented a car for the first five months following my transfer, and eventually vouchered about $1000 for the rental, a standard allowance for any transferee. Of course when the rules were set up, it was implicitly assumed that the employee was in the first stages of moving, but it was not clear to me whether I would be moving for quite some time, if ever. After several years, the accounting group asked me to return the money. I laughed at them, and kept the money. I would leave it as an exercise for my management to figure out how to handle the accounting. Eventually the accountants disappeared. The accountants would not reappear until several years later when they realized that several of us were working two shifts, but that is another, later story.

I returned to Murray Hill to work on the immediate non-working circuit problem that needed a quick solution, if that was indeed possible. I was assigned to work for A. U. (Al) Mac Rae, a supervisor with a background in the research area who was now working in Lepselter's Department.

A. U. (Al) MacRae

Al was supervisor of the Ion-Implantation Group that included some really powerful technical people. His people included Alan Moline, Jim North, Ken Pickar, Tom Seidel, and others, all experts in their craft. I was to play the role of a roving troubleshooter, with only a reputation of being hostile to incompetent management and rumored as possessing some skill at semiconductor processing development to my credit. I immediately dug into the problem that had brought me back from mediocrity, out of the anus of Allentown. My transfer from Allentown Hell back to Murray Hill (relative) Heaven was effective 15 January 1969.

David Hodges was a supervisor of the Digital Device Integration Department. He and D. J. Lyons had designed a memory cell that featured low barrier height rhodium silicide Schottky barriers as load resistors. These diode-resistors were very tiny thereby saving a lot of area, and resulted in improved performance. Lepselter had invented these devices, and with coworker J. Andrews, had previously described the characteristics of such barriers both experimentally and theoretically. Al's group was responsible for implanting the silicon directly under the Schottky diodes to a precisely predetermined value, so as to obtain the proper or designed load current.

The problem was, the circuits refused to work! Devices in lot after lot seemed to be totally inoperative! The load currents were three orders of magnitude (x1000) higher than intended. When each new set of wafers was measured and vastly elevated currents observed, Marty would look at Al and say, "I thought that you could count each ion in your machine! How did you screw up so badly?" Al would respond, "I personally watched the machine setup. There must be something else wrong!"

The situation was made vastly worse than simple error by the fact that they had already issued an abstract describing the performance features of the memory cell for delivery at the next IEEE ISSCC meeting in Philadelphia. The presentation was only a scant two months away, and the abstract had been accepted. Having to withdraw the paper would have been a black eye for both the writers and for Bell Labs. Dave Hodges was an obvious shooting star, and Lepselter was already well known and respected. MacRae's credentials were equally impeccable. In short, such a withdrawal would be a catastrophe. Careers would be damaged.

The 1969 ISSCC Best Paper Award

I went to the electrical test equipment to verify the device characteristics for myself, and set up the power supplies as specified. Sure enough, the currents were astronomical, and the circuits were completely non-functional under normal testing. Next, I examined the circuit behavior as I slowly varied the power supply, and to my surprise, found that over a very narrow voltage range, the circuits actually worked as memory cells. Upon thinking through the circuit schematic and layout as well as the very narrow voltage range resulting in functionality, I realized what the problem was! Al had **not** miscounted the ions! The Schottky loads formed the collector of unintended underlying parasitic transistors possessing very high gains, on the order of a thousand or so! The excess currents we observed were not due to implantation errors, but instead were due to the unexpected gain of underlying devices! We knew how to fix this problem using Schottky barrier diode shunts! All we had to do was kill the gain of the unintended parasitic transistors, and all would be well!

I called Marty to tell him of my discovery. According to Marty, when we discussed the finding, I looked him in the eye and announced, "The gain is just the ratio of the sheet resistances, dummy!" He immediately knew I was correct. A simple mask modification was made to kill the parasitic transistor gain, and the circuits now worked beautifully, almost exactly according to the original design. My name was added to the paper, and when the talk was given, we won the 1969 ISSCC Best Paper Award! I had validated myself and vindicated Lepselter's confidence that I could be of assistance[13]. It would remain for Al MacRae to accomplish my economic recovery with salary increases and to promote me to supervisor.

---

[13] I would guess that the Allentown boys did not realize what caused a shiver to pass through their spines.

1969 IEEE International Solid-State Circuits Conference

Outstanding Paper Award
to

H. A. Waggener

for the paper on
Low Power Bipolar Transistor
Memory Cells

Commuting and Working on the Non-Verbal Side of My Brain

Thus began the most productive period in my individual technical career. *Like an errant seed carried on the wind, I had fallen on fertile well-watered ground, and I literally blossomed.* **I had grown in my capabilities, and was once again in the company of giants!** Our combined abilities made us a powerhouse combination.

Strangely enough, the long commute was essential to my success. For the first time ever, I was forced to sit still for an hour and one half each way whether I liked it or not. I learned patience, a property I had never before exhibited. There was simply no alternative but get into the car and drive for ninety-five minutes. A second less obvious benefit was the lack of interruption. There were no visitors, no phone calls, and no interruptions, at least in good weather, so I had a lot of time to just think. I had never been primarily an analytical thinker. I usually solved most problems by deep immersion, with the non-verbal side of my brain doing most of the work. When the answer eventually became apparent, I could then describe the answer in somewhat analytical form. The long trip would give me time to both organize my day, and if the trip was boring, to solve problems while driving on autopilot.

When driving conditions were tough, that day was often not so productive.

A Black 1964 Corvair, My Supercoupe - 1969

I eventually needed to buy a car for commuting between Allentown and Murray hill, a distance of around 75 miles each way. I knew that the accountants would eventually win the arguments, so I needed an inexpensive machine and one that would offer me some ability to get back and forth regardless of the weather. Ralph Nader had written the book, "Unsafe At Any Speed" condemning the 1961 Chevrolet Corvair, and his efforts had almost killed the breed. I had read that models from 1964 on were not liable to the problems of the 1961, and so I went looking for a bargain auto hidden in plain view. I found such a car, and bought a nifty little black 1964 Corvair Coupe. There was a TV cartoon that the kids watched where the main character was a flying super chicken with super powers. I proclaimed that my trusty small vehicle was really a "Supercoupe". It served me very well for well over a year and a half. The placement of the Corvair engine over the rear drive wheels allowed the beast to move in everything but glare ice, deep snow, or high water.

Following successful identification of the parasitic transistor, Lepselter, MacRae, and I began to think about novel ways to use Schottky devices and ion implantation in device fabrication. What a wonderful time! Over the next few months, I worked on applications of Schottky barriers and application of ion implantation to fabricate novel device structures. We enlisted the aid of Herman Gummel and Sam Poon, expert theoretical device modelers, and they along with MacRae, Lepselter and I, prepared an article for presentation at 1969 Device Research Conference in Rochester NY.

Two patents were filed on behalf of Lepselter and me on 18 September 1969. Two patents were issued: Patent # 3,615,874 on 26 October 1971, and Patent # 3,617,391 on 2 November 1971.

My Next Big Achievement - Electrochemically Controlled Thinning - 1969

There was a lot of interest in the technical community at large for forming thin sheets of silicon which could be as thin as one or two microns (1/25 of one thousandth of an inch) thick, and that were suitable for various device applications. The people at Phillips of the Netherlands had invented a technique that allowed formation of such layers, but the starting material could only be a thin, almost-insulating layer grown on a substrate of opposite conductivity type. Worse, electrical defects in the starting material tended to be converted into holes in the film. Thus, while thin films of silicon made by this technique were photogenic, they had very limited utility for us.

We wanted to develop some similar technique that would be applicable to the AIM structures, which contained active devices but also required very heavily doped low-conductivity layers, the exact opposite of the films prepared by the Phillips method. If such a technique were available, then the economics of AIM structures would dramatically improve. It was already known that some etches were selective to very high concentration boron (p-type) doping, but unfortunately, the doping type was not what we needed, and it was not at all evident how the thin p-type regions could be easily incorporated into our structures. I was assigned the task of developing such a process. Ron Meek, an excellent electrochemist, had been brought on board to understand the detailed chemistry of the Phillips technique as part of this effort. It was hoped that if the process were understood at a more fundamental level, the understanding might lead to a technique more useful for us.

R. (Ron) Meek

I had long been puzzled by the annoying failure of the earliest pyrocatechol anisotropic etches to etch, and here we were looking for an etchant that stopped on a heavily doped n-type layer. I concentrated on the problem for a while. One morning, I realized that the earlier failures of the pyrocatechol system to etch were due to stray unintended potentials resulting from the battery formed between the silicon and exposed metallization on the edge of the wafer. In short, I realized that since the pyrocatechol had an <u>extremely</u> low oxide etch rate on silicon dioxide, even a slight positive potential would grow a thin oxide, and silicon etching would essentially stop. I further realized that by placing p-n junctions within in the substrate, exactly predictable etch stops could be easily obtained! I was ecstatic! I allowed the idea to marinate for a few hours to see if I could find a hole in my thinking, but could find none. Late that afternoon, I called

Marty and exclaimed, "I have the solution to the thinning problem, literally as well as figuratively!" He said he would come over as soon as he was through eating dinner and soon arrived at my lab.

I excitedly told Marty about my insight, and described the details. I explained to him that the alkali etches dissolved silicon chemically, liberating hydrogen gas. That is, no external electrons needed to be supplied to make the reaction go. However, if the silicon were to be attached to a positive potential, then an anodic oxide could be made to grow, and since the oxide thus grown dissolved slowly in this class of etches, the silicon etching could be controlled very precisely. I drew pictures using simple circuit theory to describe the principles further, and the more detailed mechanisms responsible for silicon removal in both the fast and slow etching states. As I talked, Marty's eyes glazed over and he said, "I don't really understand much about chemistry. If you are right, this problem is solved!" and he went home to relax.

Within a day or two I had a p type silicon wafer deep-diffused (in the model shop) with phosphorous giving a junction depth of around 20 microns, well within the needed range, and had the diffused sample prepared for etching. I deposited titanium gold metals onto the diffused wafer and a matching portion of a sapphire disc. I mounted the wafer with the smooth diffused side down onto the sapphire disc using the Tyler AIM mounting material, and made sure that there was electrical continuity between the wafer and disc. I grabbed the metallized sapphire disc with a zirconium clip, placed the wafer/disc sandwich into my KOH AIM etching station, using a platinum screen as a second electrode. With no external potential applied to the silicon, copious hydrogen bubble evolution demonstrated rapid etching activity. When I raised the potential above some critical value, the bubble evolution would immediately cease, indicating that etching had stopped or had at least considerably slowed. It was now apparent to me that by carefully adjusting the voltage, I could retain the desired n-type region while the reverse bias junction between the n and p regions would allow the p-type substrate to etch away!

I called Marty's office, and he immediately came down to my lab. I showed him the setup, with the silicon rapidly liberating hydrogen bubbles as it dissolved. "How long will it take?" he asked nervously. "About three hours." I replied. He waited around for about an hour or so, and said something like, "I can't stand the suspense. I have to go home! Call me if it works!" After another couple of hours, the bubbles stopped coming off parts of the wafer, as I expected. I called Marty at home and said it looked good. He only lived a couple of blocks away, and immediately came over, in time to see the last of the bubbling cease as only the heavily doped n region remained. The wafer hung on the clip, a uniform deep reddish-brown color, since it was now thin enough to partially transmit red light! What a beautiful sight!

We went off to have a drink and celebrate this momentous step forward!

In the meantime, late in 1969 Jim Early left the Labs to take the helm of Fairchild. As he himself had once told me about some such moves, I thought that the managerial skills at both institutions were both thereby improved. I had no doubt that Jim Early was an early giant, and an important contributor to semiconductor practice and understanding. The only question in my mind was his timely managerial judgment.

When Jim Early left Allentown, The old Allentown Alliance of Questionable Individuals had grown increasingly hostile towards Lepselter and his assorted technologies, including beam leads and AIM. They had a laundry list of complaints regarding a number of items, and had apparently chosen AIM as a point of easy attack. I would guess that they hoped to win on this point and thereby undermine Lepselter's credibility, and so on.

The attack had been elevated to the extent that Jack Morton held a technology review in Murray Hill in order to resolve outstanding issues and differences. The Allentown crew went through their list of laments. I was later told that they eventually got around to the issue of AIM, and how difficult and expensive it was to achieve thickness control. In rebuttal, Marty held up the thin, uniform layer remaining after electrochemically controlled thinning, exhibiting a uniform dark red wafer still supported on the sapphire carrier. He outlined the very simple thinning process, and their attack balloon was immediately deflated! QED

At some point later on in the festivities, Morton and a gaggle of department heads toured our facilities, including my lab in 2B209, where I had a demonstration wafer etching merrily away. Morton made some comments and asked how I thought this development would influence the AIM process. I commented that, "If we ever get serious, this will make an enormous difference, both in control and in economics". He looked shocked, and immediately asked, "What, aren't we really serious now?" "No, I don't think so." I said. He looked at me, somewhat startled, and shortly thereafter left the room. The remaining remnants of worried department heads breathed a collective sigh of relief. Morton had left the room and had gone without piercing their sides. Better yet, their intestines were still on the inside of their bodies. The assembled gaggle of supervisors and department heads would live to breathe and collect paychecks yet another day!

Lepselter had become a prodigious contributor to the field, with many accomplishments to his credit. Marty was soon offered promotion from Department Head in Murray Hill to Director of the Allentown Laboratory, the position previously vacated by Jim Early's departure. I like to think that I helped Marty's cause on that day of Morton's review, at least a little. I recall several days of his soul searching when Marty and I would walk the Murray Hill grounds discussing what the future might hold. He wisely accepted the promotion in late 1969. I was happy for him, but felt that I would lose contact with a really close friend. We would no longer be able to interact in the same way. I really felt the loss.

Al MacRae Becomes my Mentor and Champion – Late 1969

Al MacRae was promoted to Department Head, replacing Lepselter. Alan Moline was promoted to supervisor of the Ion Implantation Group, a wholly warranted move. I still reported to MacRae, and found that my environment continued to be extremely supportive. Al let me handle the assignments of one of his groups, remnants of Lepselter's earlier gang. This gang included Joe Ligenza, physical chemist; who I have mentioned before, Fred Koch, metallurgist; Pete Byrnes, and W. Polito.

P. A. (Pete) Byrnes

W. Polito

In these days, I would arrive at work from my roadway meditations, and immediately circulate among members of the group resetting their efforts for the day. Only when I was satisfied with their progress would I either find Al, or work on my own stuff.

Al had been a researcher in Area 1, and had a number of accomplishments to his credit. His parents had grown up in Canada, but he was born in Syracuse and as a boy earned his spurs as a paperboy in Providence Rhode Island, and Syracuse New York. Al was therefore a first class researcher as well as a skilled intellectual street fighter. He was a pleasure to work with: strong, insistent, and highly motivational. We continued to be close friends and coworkers. He was also an artful and skillful leader.

Al took it upon himself to get me recognition, and to repair my image. He knew that I needed to publish my work on silicon thinning, would not let me wiggle away, and sort of twisted my arm so that I would write a short article for publication. The article was published as a Bell System Technical Journal (BSTJ) Brief, "Electrochemically Controlled Thinning of Silicon", H. A. Waggener, Bell System Technical Journal, Volume 49, March 1970, Number 7. On 4 April 1970, I presented a talk to the Allentown technical staff, covering the general material discussed in the BSTJ article in a little more detail. I don't remember much about the talk. I think that Marty appreciated it, as did some of my earlier supporters, while from my earlier opponents, all that was heard was the sound of one hand clapping. At least after this particular talk, I had only a short ride home. I have inserted a copy of the BSTJ article below:

B.S.T.J. BRIEF
Electrochemically Controlled Thinning of Silicon
By H. A. WAGGENER

(Manuscript received December 31, 1969)

A method for precision thinning silicon integrated circuit slices has been developed whereby either n or p type regions may be selectively removed from material of opposite conductivity. The existence of a simple and economical means to attain precise thickness control permits more complete advantage to be taken of many silicon IC structures. For example, precise thickness control, together with anisotropic[1] etching of isolation/separation slots, is expected to permit economical fabrication of high component density, air-isolated monolithic[2] integrated circuits.

This method differs from previous electrochemical techniques[3] in that unwanted silicon is removed chemically, while the regions to be retained are passivated electrochemically. Accordingly, etchants are used for which silicon to be retained is passive when biased above some critical voltage, V_{pass}, while regions to be removed are at a potential below V_{pass}.

Hot aqueous alkaline solutions form a useful class of etchants for this application, for orientations other than (111). These etchants are characterized by a relatively sharp active/passive transition ($V_{cell} = V_{pass} \approx 0.5$ volt) and by a large ratio of silicon etch rates between the active and passive states. Ratios of greater than 200 : 1 are readily obtained. The ratio of active etch rate/passive etch rate is very important, because this quantity in part determines the thickness uncertainty.

Application of the technique to the formation of thin, uniformly thick n type silicon slices is illustrated in Fig. 1. If $V_{cell} > V_{pass}$, then $V_n = V_{cell} > V_{pass}$ and the n region will be retained. If V_{cell} is restricted to voltages such that the leakage of the reverse biased junction is

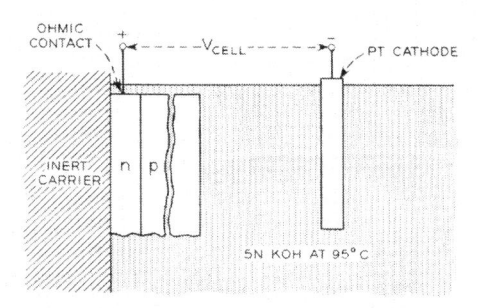

Fig. 1 — Schematic illustration of the thinning technique as used to form n type slices with accurately controlled thickness. An n region is formed by epitaxy or by diffusion. The starting material is high-resistivity p material. When the cell is biased as described in the text, the p region can be removed while the n region is retained. Neither the exact composition nor temperature of the etching solution is critical.

sufficiently small, then $V_p < V_{pass}$, and the p region will be removed. It is assumed that the contacts are arranged so that the lateral ohmic drop in the n type silicon is small enough to be negligible.

For the cell arrangement shown, V_{pass} is about 0.5 volt for either n or p material. Thus thin p-type slices can be formed by reversing the location of the n and p layers as shown in Fig. 2. The maximum allowable cell voltage is reduced because the controlling junction is now forward biased.

Structures of this type have been made where the n layer was formed by diffusion into a background approximately 2.5×10^{-2} cm thick.

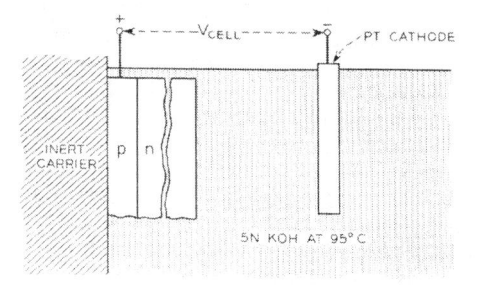

Fig. 2 — Schematic illustration of the thinning technique as used to form p type slices with accurately controlled thickness. Cell polarity is unchanged.

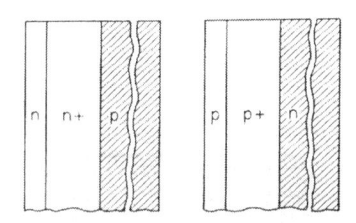

Fig. 3 — Multilayered structures which can be fabricated using the thinning technique. These structures are particularly suitable for making npn and pnp integrated circuits.

After thinning, the difference between the thickness of the remaining n layer and the depth of the diffusion was about 3×10^{-5} cm.

Multilayered structures can also be fabricated as illustrated in Fig. 3. These structures are particularly suitable for fabrication of npn and pnp air-isolated or dielectric-isolated integrated circuits. The thickness control is determined by the combined thickness of the diffused and epitaxial layers, and is expected to be easily controllable to within 10 percent.

Experimental beam leaded, air-isolated monolithic integrated circuits have been made on n/n+/p starting material and have been thinned by the technique described. A total of approximately 2.5×10^{-2} cm of p material was removed in one step, without prior mechanical operations.

REFERENCES

1. Waggener, H. A., Kragness, R. C., and Tyler, A. L., "Anisotropic Etching for Forming Isolation Slots in Silicon Beam Leaded Integrated Circuits," IEEE International Electron Devices Meeting, Washington, D. C., October 19, 1967 (talk).
2. Lepselter, M. P., "Beam Lead Technology," B.S.T.J., 45, No. 2 (February 1966), pp. 233–253.
3. Dutch patent No 67030B, Aug 26, 1968.

Al and I continued to churn out ideas concerning novel device structures and methods of fabricating them. The long meditation time in my Supercoupe was continuing to pay off! I had been on a roll, and I kept on rolling, both literally and figuratively.

Enter John Dalton and Room 1E358 – Mid 1970

It soon became evident to Al and me that we needed to have a small processing facility to service the needs of his department. Such a facility would make experimentation much easier than using the existing facilities, and since it would be under our direct control, cajoling and politicking to get the necessary time would be totally avoided. It was apparent that we could use a talented process-oriented individual to run the place. One day an opportunity arose to acquire draft rights for John V. Dalton, but Al had to trade a supervisory group to land him.

J. V. (John) Dalton

Al also negotiated for a two-bay long room, 1E358, on the third floor of Building 1, about three quarters of a mile from my office. It was distant, but it would do! John and I soon outfitted the room with a complement of small furnaces, cleaning stations, as well as photo-resist application and exposure equipment. The room was absolutely stuffed to overflowing, a veritable semiconductor processing sausage, sort of like the kitchen of a small trailer home.

John Dalton was a perfect choice for the task. He had extensive processing experience, was of superior intelligence, and had a marvelous even-tempered personality. He was also scrupulously honest and not prone to exaggeration or deceit. In addition, we liked and respected each other. This little facility would be complete late in the year, and was to be invaluable to the larger Murray Hill semiconductor effort in the future.

Among other things, John was to help characterize the EC thinning process. He found a high temperature wax for mounting wafers to be thinned in non-alcoholic KOH solutions, prepared samples and participated in the measurements. His work was invaluable. A patent application was filed on 15 December 1969. We prepared an abstract for a talk on Electrochemically Controlled Thinning for presentation at the Atlantic City Electrochemical Society 1970. Patent #3,689,389, "Electrochemically Controlled Shaping of Semiconductors" issued 5 September 1972.

Al continued to provide me strong but constructive guidance, and we often discussed technical matters over beer and pizza. On one such afternoon, I had an inspiration for a patentable idea, and while we were eating, I sketched the idea on a used paper plate stained with runoff from my pizza. Al witnessed and understood the slippery plate, and the next Monday, I submitted the paper plate, grease, and all, to the patent group. The patent people dutifully placed the unusual document into their official files! Al later got the comment that this method of communication with the patent group was unique in their history. This form of communication had not been used heretofore. Al and I both thought that it was not only a good idea, but we had good fun as well! I don't recall whether the idea was worthwhile (i.e. patentable) or not.

Sigurd Waaben and His Two-Diode Memory - 1970

Shortly after the TM for electrochemically controlled thinning had circulated, I was approached by Sigurd Waaben, who worked in an exploratory memory group in MH, to possibly participate in a new application of Schottky and charge-storage diodes to make memory devices.

S. (Sigurd) Waaben

The architecture of Sigurd's two-diode memory was ideal for the advanced AIM structures now possible. He explained the desired structures to me and I agreed to join in his effort. I laid out the circuits to make a 16-bit test array, had the masks made, and had the devices processed by the model shop, up to the thinning steps.

I completed the EC thinning steps using the mounting material developed by Tyler in Allentown, followed by the alignment and etch-apart steps. The arrays fabricated using the **EC thinning technique, my first Masterpiece,** were beautiful! They were glistening small gems, fabricated quickly, easily, and at high yields!

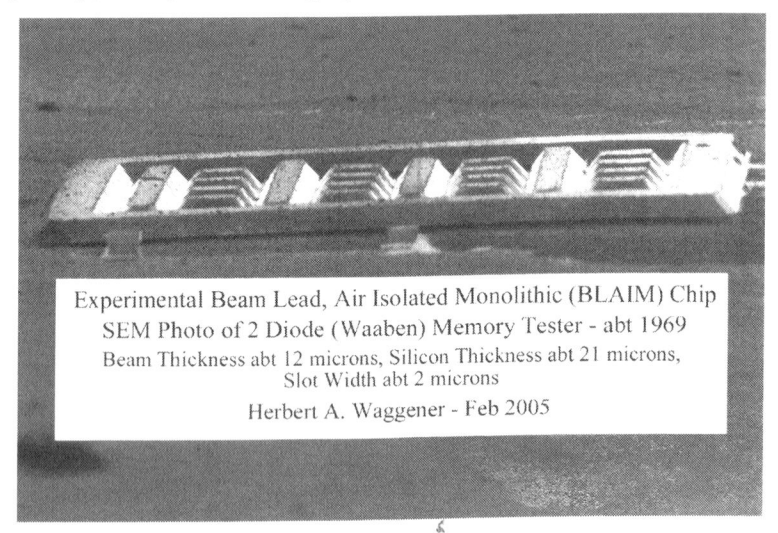

Experimental Beam Lead, Air Isolated Monolithic (BLAIM) Chip
SEM Photo of 2 Diode (Waaben) Memory Tester - abt 1969
Beam Thickness abt 12 microns, Silicon Thickness abt 21 microns, Slot Width abt 2 microns
Herbert A. Waggener - Feb 2005

Each little die had precisely controlled thickness, had precisely aligned slots, and each slot was a work of perfection! THE WHOLE PACKAGE WORKED IN TOTO! There had been no mechanical stress on thinning, no precision mechanical polishing step, no worry about the final thickness, and no concern about the quality of slot etching. We removed the mounting material with ozone in my lab, and had random samples bonded onto previously prepared ceramic substrates for test. Sigurd took the mounted chips away, and after a little while, I got a call telling me to come over to his lab and take a look! The devices worked exactly as he had predicted! We had successfully implemented his new invention!

Sigurd wrote the TM describing the two-diode memory concept, and I continued to process a few devices, making a new set of masks and eventually fabricating working arrays of 128 bits each. I made an exploratory array comprising a die containing nine sub-arrays containing 128 bits each to illustrate how the technology could be scaled up while still allowing protection against silicon fracture. The larger array was essentially pre-broken and therefore quite durable. An article was eventually published: "100 ns Electronically Variable Semiconductor Memory Using Two Diodes Per Memory Cell", IEEE Journal of Solid State Circuits, Vol. SC-5, October 1970.

There was also a press release regarding the two-diode memory technology. I have reproduced the cover from the 23 January 1971 Business Week magazine, on the next page.

Business Week Cover, 23 January 1971. Elements of the Waaben memory array are visible under the Bell, a nice display.

Silicon on Insulator

In July of 1970, Director David G. Thomas asked me to comment on an article. I include excerpts from the cover letter and my attached response below:

Mr. W. S. Boyle:

David Thomas has asked me to comment on an article in the Wall Street Journal. Attached please find my comments, which you may find suitable for forwarding to J. Morton.

H. A. Waggener

Copy to

Messrs. CG B. Garret
    A. U. MacRae
    D. G. Thomas

"In view of the materials restrictions imposed by growing silicon on an insulator, it seems desirable to invert the process and form the insulator on thin silicon. The net result is a separation of variables and a relaxation of requirements on the various materials.

To do this, silicon would be epitaxially grown on a silicon substrate, with subsequent formation of the insulating layer(s) (fig. 1 and 2). Removal of the silicon substrate by electrochemical techniques results in formation of the basic silicon structure. Material quality is now not determined by the insulating substrate, so that either bipolar or thin MOS devices can be made within the same general technology".

> *In view of the above, the desirable device structure, thin silicon on an insulator can be made using a technology more general than "silicon on sapphire". It is recommended that dielectric isolation using self-stopping techniques be developed for high-speed applications. Such efforts are underway in Dept ----".*
>
> *H. A. Waggener*

With the ability to reliably (and inexpensively) form thin layers of device quality silicon on an insulator of predetermined characteristics, and to have access to the reverse side of the device structure was an exciting possibility. Excellent solid dielectric or air isolation now became almost trivial. Any possible four-layer CMOS latch up also disappeared. It did not look like we would work ourselves out of a job in the near future. In the meantime, I had a few more details to take care of.

More Electrochemistry - That Silicon Has Potential! – Late 1970

When I had applied a positive voltage to the silicon for the thinning operation, I used a platinum mesh as a negative electrode. Thus, I knew the potential on the silicon and the mesh, but I had no knowledge of the potential of the solution itself. For the thinning operation, it was unnecessary to have such knowledge, because the margins were large. For my next project, I would need a precise knowledge of the etchant potential. An electrochemist whose name I can't remember, told me to use a **"reference electrode"** composed of a one molar KOH solution against a solid mixture of mercuric oxide/mercury/platinum wire to measure the potential. I wanted to determine the dependence of silicon etch rates upon the (etching) solution-to-silicon potential, and now I was in a position to do so.

Pages from my notebook dated 13 November 1970 record the concept and plots of measured etch rates vs. potentials. I found that I could now precisely determine the relative ratios of (100) and (110) etch rates without recourse to an accident resulting from the effects of various alcohols. **<u>For the first time, I had electrical control of all the important etching variables</u>**. The thickness of the AIM structure was controlled by the placement of a junction, the location of the major slot walls were controlled by the crystal itself and the lithographic printing step, and the corners were controlled by an additional variable, the solution-to-silicon potential.

Our facility in 1E358 was finished and became available for more general use. John Dalton and I fabricated the etching samples used to determine the slot etching characteristics as discussed above. I wrote up a technical memorandum describing the results, and following our total immersion in a massive effort called Phase 2, which I will describe shortly, eventually wrote an abstract and presented the talk at the Miami Beach, October 1972 ECS meeting.

In August 1970, I authored a TM, "AIM Layout and Design for Experimental Circuits, and in November 1970, co-authored another TM, "Process Instructions for Air Isolated Monolithic Circuits" with Bob MacDonald, who had also coauthored the original beam lead paper with Lepselter in 1964. These memoranda were written to encourage designers to use AIM for their designs, and to encourage the Allentown process groups to incorporate these improvements into their flow sheets.

All this meant that among other things, I had devised the world's most precise three-dimensional machining capability, and it was resident in my fume hood! These structures were controlled to within a micron or two in each major dimension! Not only that, but the process was easy, reproducible, and inexpensive!

The general setup is shown on the following page. This particular quartz flask would hold around a liter of etchant, and was therefore limited to 2 in diameter wafers, the largest then in use by us. An illustration similar to this is reproduced on the back cover of this book.

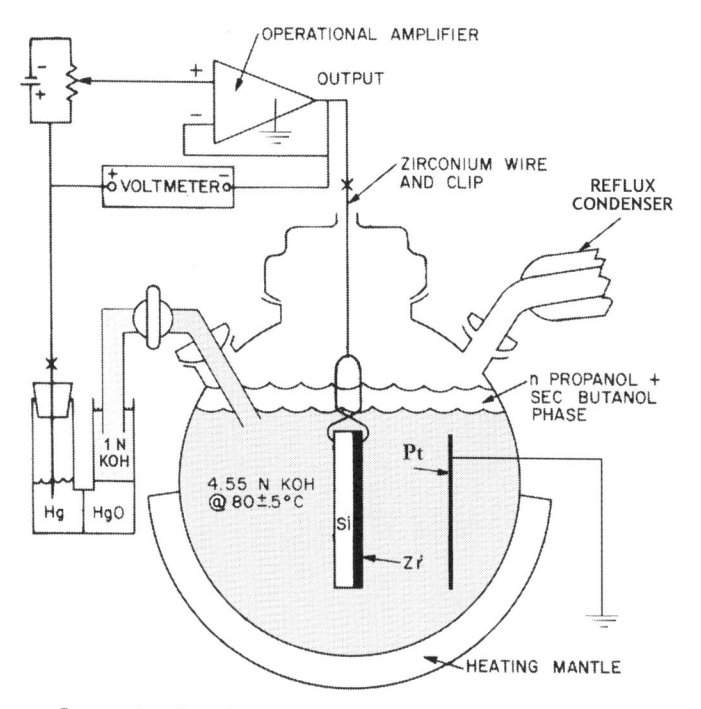

Setup for Precise Potentiometric Silicon Etching
The world's most precise three dimensional shaping
in 1970 existed in my fume hood - haw 2009.

On 18 March 1971, C. G. B. Garret requested a patent study, "controlling anisotropic etch rates with applied potential and with additives", but no patent was ever applied for. I suspect that the eventual lack of interest foretold the soon-to-be preoccupation with MOS devices, and possibly a diminished interest in large-scale bipolar integrated circuits.

My Promotion to Supervisor - December 1970

In a little less than two years since I had escaped Allentown, my star had risen high enough into the sky to be

197

promoted to supervisor. Al had done his work well, and made me supervisor of the "Metal, Oxide, and Semiconductor Group", reporting to him. As he said, "You have been directing the activities of that group for a couple of years. It was time to give you the title." In essence, we could work on any project we found interesting. The group consisted of Fred Koch, Joe Ligenza, Pete Byrnes, John Dalton, Bill Polito, and Bill Powell. Sam Broydo was to soon join my group to round out the powerhouse.

With the promotion came another raise in salary. Since I had first returned to Murray Hill, my raises now totaled over 37%, and life was becoming more affordable. Both my family I and had some financial relief, but the price was considerable. During the week, I scarcely saw my little crew of stalwarts. Probably the most obviously effected was my son Mark. When I had worked in Allentown, I had been helping coach the Emmaus Pop Warner football team after work hours, and while I was working at Murray Hill, I would not see him at all on most workdays. I would normally leave very early, and get home late. It was harder to tell what effect the long hours away had on twins John and Shawn. If they were bothered, I couldn't see it, and they didn't tell me so.

In retrospect, I doubt that my explanation as to why I was no longer always around didn't really make much sense to them. Frankly, it didn't make a whole lot of sense to me either.

Sam Broydo – Physicist, Superb Analyst, and Friend – Early 1971

Sam Broydo joined my group around this time. Sam was to become my third great friend and ally in my up-and-down-and-up career at Bell Labs. After this interlude, our paths would cross a number of times in several interesting ways.

Samuel (Sam) Broydo

Sam had received a PhD in England, where his thesis was on hetrojunction devices. He was offered a job at Bell Labs in Murray Hill, and arrived in this country in about 1966, together with his beautiful wife, Lina, and son Mark. He and I would find that our skills were extremely complementary. He was a superb analyst, and I was a pretty darn good subliminal problem solver, truly a **Sorcerer's Apprentice**!

My processing facility was paying dividends. Group activities included fabrication of thin silicon and AIM structures for me, working on the effects of process variables influencing guarded Schottky diode properties for use in innovative structures, and included evaluation of oxides grown by Joe Ligenza in his oxygen plasma. John Dalton and Ken Pickar of Moline's group developed cleaning, oxidation, implant, and annealing schedules to produce nearly ideal Picturephone^R targets.

Sam Broydo, John Dalton, and I began looking at the properties of gate oxides. According to Sam, right after he joined me, I showed him an article written by R. J. Krieger of Bell Northern Research, concerning oxides grown in atmospheres of O2 (oxygen) and HCl (hydrochloric acid) vapor. The basic notion was that the HCl would react with contaminants in the oxidation system while growing oxide films, possibly resulting in oxides with superior quality. Kriegler had grown some oxides, but his oxides possessed very dubious properties, and strangely, his oxides were apparently bulletproof with respect to sodium contamination. Some industry people thought that this latter "bulletproof" property was very troublesome, indicating something very badly wrong.

We thought that such oxides might result in superior gate oxides if carefully done. This was soon to be verified. Our oxides were sodium free, stable, and showed excellent dielectric properties. Better yet, they were not in any way resistant to sodium contamination. These oxides were of excellent quality in every respect! The metal contaminant levels in the silicon itself were also improved, so it appeared that we had been right, **everything** was cleaner. This and similar oxidation sequences and conditions were to soon become standard throughout the Bell System and elsewhere.

Our situation with regard to innovative processing was almost perfect, but both Murray Hill and Allentown semiconductor activities were soon to be totally redirected. High-level management belatedly came to the realization that our Bell semiconductor technology implementation was in a very, very poor state. Without Jack Morton, change was not only possible, but also necessary.

Pete Panousis and a Fortuitous Hallway Technical Meeting Early 1971

I had known Pete Panousis from earlier times in Murray Hill. We had never worked directly together, but we had numerous discussions, and we both respected each other's abilities. He had been transferred to Allentown a little earlier, and I had heard that he was working on a severe problem with the nitride junction-seal process. The Western Electric production lines were shut down, because the product being made was unreliable, about the worst situation possible.

One day I stopped by the Allentown Facility to say hello to Lepselter, now the Allentown Bell Labs Director. By chance, I found Pete in the hallway, and we stopped to talk. I asked him causally, "What is the problem?" Pete explained that one of the necessary etching steps was leaving a ledge of silicon nitride around the contact holes. Sodium contaminants could not be reliably removed from under these ledges. Attempts to etch the ledge away had failed, as the only known nitride etch also often etched some of the device areas away. My eyes brightened, and I said, "That's simple, **add sulfuric acid** to the etch. The sulfuric acid will prevent the silicon from dissolving, so that your approach will work." Pete replied, "I'll try it". With a sigh he walked away heading for his lab.

The next day, I got an excited call from Pete. "It works! It works!" he said. He indicated that a little further work was needed, but it looked like this answer was adequate to resolve the problem. He expected to allow production to proceed very soon. Solving a line-stopping problem **not** of

202

your own making is about the best thing that can be done in a manufacturing environment, provided that you are not invisible. **Pete was an Allentown HERO!**

Pete could have easily taken full credit for the solution, since there was no written record of our hallway encounter, nor were there any witnesses. Pete demonstrated considerable character and moral fiber. We jointly wrote up the technical memorandum describing the problem and the solution. A patent was filed on 3 September 1971, and patent # 3,715,249, "Si_3N_4 Etching", was issued on 6 February 1973. I did not know it at the time, but the five-minute conversation that led to this accomplishment would at least partially save me from total financial ruin at the next joint Allentown-Murray Hill merit review later in the year.

Tag and Judy at Jersey Shore, Allentown Era

Tag and Sam at Jersey Shore, Allentown Era

Mom and Dad Return to Appleton City, 1971

During the summer, my Mom and Dad moved from what had been our semi-permanent home in Lakeside to Appleton City Missouri. Horace and Grace Alexander had previously moved from Rockville to take up residence there. Mother and Grace had been good friends for years, and so it was decided to return to this part of the state. Mom and Dad bought the house at 303 East 2nd Street, directly across the street from the Alexander home. The two-story house was in need of some considerable renovation. Horace was an excellent carpenter and would be of considerable help when the house was renovated.

The renovation process would prove to be rather extensive. My brother Bud and I decided to help. We arranged our vacations so that our families could be there at the same time. Bud brought a large camping tent to ease the sleeping problem but otherwise we simply had to make do. Six adults and six children made for interesting sleeping and eating logistics.

The restoration work was HOT, hard, long, and tiring. The exterior of the house had been built on a combination stone/concrete foundation wall, with smaller piers supporting the interior floors and walls. The exterior foundations were in pretty good shape, but the interior piers had long ago settled, causing the floors to be lower in the center, and for the central brick chimney to be several inches lower than intended. The subsidence was in fact largely caused by the weight of the chimney sitting on an inadequate support pier.

For our first step, we began dismantling the chimney so that the interior of the house could be safely lifted with jacks, and the piers rebuilt. Now, in addition to the heat and other aspects, mortar and brick dust filled out shirts and lungs. The work was hard, but soon the yard outside was piled with bricks, and the chimney was gone. Men had been hired to perform the actual jacking operation, and by carefully using additional supporting temporary joists and large construction jacks, the interior walls were nudged back to where they were intended. Since the weight of the chimney was gone, installing simple shims on the existing piers completed this part of the job. Both my brother and I were happy that this phase was done.

The next steps included refurbishing the bathroom and kitchen, repairing cracked interior walls, fixing holes in the ceiling plaster upstairs, reworking some of the electrical system and other general fixing up, including rebuilding the front porch and reflashing part of the roof. Horace Alexander had been invaluable in the repairs. When we were done, we were glad that we had been able to lend a hand. Dad would continue to work on the place in times to come, but the place was clearly livable when our vacations ended forcing us to return to our employment.

Repair Crew: Horace Alexander, Dad, Buddy, and Me
303 E. 2nd Street, Appleton City MO. - 1971

Meanwhile, any plans I had to develop Silicon-On-Insulator technology were put on indefinite hold due to new directions back in Murray Hill. I would not get another opportunity to do this development until the 1980's when I was at the Teletype Corporation in Skokie Illinois, but this effort too would have to be abandoned when Teletype was closed down.

Chapter 6 - New Directions for Semiconductor Development

Phase 1 and Phase 2 are Defined – May 1971

David Thomas was promoted to Executive Director, and C. G. B. (Geoffrey) Garret took his place as our Director, thereby becoming Department Head Al MacRae's boss. Apparently there was some grand powwow at stratospheric levels where it was recognized that something had to be done to improve the level of execution in our semiconductor production facilities, and we needed to use Bell Lab's vaunted intellectual power to leapfrog past the silicon gate, aluminum metallization technology being implemented by outside industries like Intel, Texas Instruments, and Motorola.

This leaping, by us technology frogs, was to be accomplished in two parts, named Phase 1 and Phase 2.

Although the phases were numbered consecutively, they were in fact to run concurrently.

Phase 1 would be headed by Marty Lepselter in Allentown. Phase 1 would address the level of execution for all Allentown and Reading Western Electric facilities producing integrated circuits, as well as development facilities at these locations belonging to Bell Labs. The goal was to bring the production lines to at least the level of our nominal external competitors.

Phase 2 was to be lead by Geoffrey Garret in Murray Hill. This goal, as explained to me, was to leapfrog past any technology then being practiced by our competitors. The general thought was that after successful implementation of Phases 1 and 2, the advanced technology would be transferred into production forthwith, leaving the Bell System semiconductor production beyond industry parity (as befits the assembled talent pool, arguably the best in the world). Both Phase 1 and Phase 2 were to have the full support of whatever resources were internally available. This was to be a do-or-die operation, and we were sure that we did not want to die.

C. G. B. (Goeffry) Garret

Garrett assembled his minions and explained how Phase 2 was going to work. He explained that he had chosen a tactic unusual for Bell Labs. Geoffrey personally dictated the specific structure that he wanted fabricated and the materials to be used as well. The structure he desired took an impressive number of adjectives to describe. As he explained, "Normally, people at Bell Labs invent structures to circumvent fabrication problems. Since I have defined the Structure, I want you to invent ways to make it." I don't remember the details of his announced plan, but he announced the general rules of engagement he was going to follow. These rules were:

1. The staff would be organized into teams reporting directly to him, regardless of individual rank or title, and he would specify the team members.

2. Geoffrey would personally preside at each team meeting, on a schedule that he would determine, but he would sit with each team at least weekly.

3. There would be an additional weekly "hot spot" meeting where he and David Thomas would preside and relevant Department Heads would be present. This meeting would concentrate on areas that needed special attention and/or pressure beyond that afforded by the regular meetings. This meeting came to be held on Monday mornings.

4. Geoffrey and only Geoffrey would change the rules as needed.

5. R. Buckley would be use his facility and operate it as our pilot production line.

6. We would start immediately.

As Garrett explained, "We spend over 150 million dollars annually on our semiconductor development, which is more than the total value of the integrated circuits we make each year. 150 million dollars can buy an awful lot of devices from our competitors! Do you understand what I am telling you? Get busy or look for other work." David Thomas did his best to look menacing and stern, but was otherwise silent.

It was said that within one day, a representative of RCA Corporation of Somerville NJ appeared at our front door with a quote to supply all the semiconductor products then in manufacture by Western Electric. The quote included delivery schedules and pre-negotiated prices, all of which seemed reasonable. The annual dollar value of the quote was for a lot less than 150 million dollars/year. Apparently, someone(s) inside Bell had previously supplied RCA people with all the information needed to work up the quote. I never heard whether the information leakers were found or if they even really existed. Such was my confidence in higher management and their utterances.

The Phase 2 Structure is Revealed - May 1971

The words needed to describe the structure Garrett had described included a list of adjectives a yard long. I will try to list them all only once before mostly ignoring them all. I will not use the adjectives that had to be added, due to later experience. I recite this listing to give a sense of the complexity and a sense of the verbiage. Besides featuring the use of chemically unstable refractory metal tungsten as the gate material, the picture Geoffrey had drawn featured the following items: Implanted channel stops under the field oxide; (undeveloped) tungsten deposition: self-aligned first level tungsten gate metal: implanted source-drains; a (undeveloped) vapor-deposited intermediate oxide; a second level tungsten interconnection level; an unknown sodium and heavy metal gettering technique; an unknown capping oxide passivation level; unknown annealing schedules; with unknown device design rules; an unknown substrate contact; and an unknown configuration for final assembly. What could be simpler?

There was little question in my mind that the structure could be built. It was only a matter of working out the details. I coined the phrase, **"Of course the Grand Scheme will work. Only the details might not be achievable"**. I would use this phrase often in the years to come. It seemed unlikely that we would be able to outperform a well-established commercial industry from our little fiefdom, whatever our assembled intellectual might. It would turn out that while we did some good work, we were a little short of whelming the world with our clever machinations.

The people who would comprise the teams were assigned, meetings began to be held, and equipment and materials ordered. As promised, Geoffrey chaired each normal meeting, making sure that things were progressing as desired. Al MacRae was serving as chief technical advisor to Garrett, and was usually present in these meetings.

"Hot-Seat" meetings were also held, and according to what I heard, became implements of torture for those unfortunate enough to be summoned thereto. Being "on the carpet" was a poor representation of the tone and manner of conduct. More than one weasel was skewered and cooked in these fires. Repeated weasel wasting also became a routine practice

Among the early things Phase 2 needed were devices suitable for testing the various components of the technology. The design groups began to generate test designs and get them converted into photolithography masks needed for processing. The process-related groups also began turning on their equipment to implement the laundry list needed to make the Phase 2 structure. As soon as the basic techniques were worked out, R. Buckley's line began repetitive processing, working on reproducibility, and marching to a schedule. Unfortunately the road turned out to be a little rocky, and needed some major boulders removed.

Sam and John Dalton, using our facility in 1E358, were able to routinely demonstrate only slightly contaminated oxide-metal structures using standard aluminum metallization. After the initial work showed such promise, Sam had a one-man garage-type firm, MTI Inc., build a new gas panel to his specifications, much cleaner and more professional than the home-built previous one. MTI went on the sell a number of these panels to Intel, IBM, and others by saying something like, "This is the latest design out of Bell Labs". When the oxidation furnace heating elements burned out, Sam drove to the furnace supplier's warehouse, brought a new one back to the labs in his car trunk, carried it up to 1E358, and it was reinstalled. The furnace was back on line within a day and requalified with a minimum of downtime.

Bill Polito was soon able to routinely deposit clean, adherent films of tungsten metal that were free of sodium, thereby confirming overall purity. Danny MacCahan, MTS in a sister department, had the only Kuhn-Silversmith sodium measurement system that was readily available.

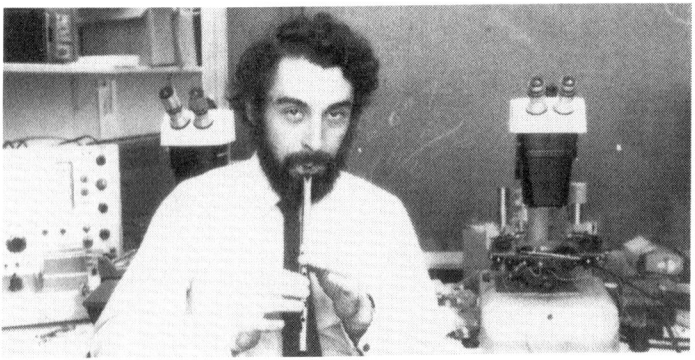

D. (Danny) MacCahan

Originally, Sam used Danny's equipment at night, since Danny used it during the day. Bill Powell duplicated the test equipment for oxide contamination measurements to remove the bottleneck. Sam then used this equipment almost exclusively for Phase 2 evaluations. Sam was now in a position to use our oxides to qualify individual steps in other areas. He did so, and this effort was essential to this phase of the process shakedown. In the meantime, I had to find another vehicle for my lengthy commute.

I Upgrade to a Canary Yellow 1965 Corvair

The many miles had been taking their toll on my trusty Supercoupe. Corvairs used diverted engine cooling air to provide heat for the passenger compartment. This was fine, except that as the o-rings began to harden with time, oil began leaking past the hardened o-rings to vaporize on hot engine exhaust manifolds. This in turn led to oil vapors being included in the heated air. As the miles had quickly built up, driving the Supercoupe simply became untenable. I was still deeply engrossed in becoming a truly useful performer at work, and had not yet seriously taken up the task of maintaining my automobiles. Thus, I looked for a later model Corvair and found a dandy 4-door sedan, somewhat the color of a canary. The price was right, the condition was excellent and best of all, the o-rings were still good, so that the passenger compartment no longer smelled like an oil refinery.

This was a snappy-looking car! Not only was the car good-looking, the 1965 model now had a suspension system previously used in only a few sports cars. The weight distribution remained primarily over the rear drive wheels so vehicle traction was unchanged, and the road ability was now truly outstanding. The handling characteristics of this car would save my life on at least one occasion in the near future. I would drive this car for several years, even after I left Bell Labs to work at Teletype in Skokie Illinois in 1973.

I Am "Invited" to the Hot-Seat Meeting, a New Platform

There were many decisions being made in the Hot Seat meetings regarding disposition of troops and process machinery that I simply could not understand. One day I was called into such a meeting to answer some question that had arisen. Having been asked to come to a conclusion, I was required to attend the meetings until management was satisfied with resolution of the matter. I was therefore required to attend several meetings, and observe the goings on. I soon discovered that the terrified participants were telling our leaders what they thought would take the pressure off rather than the truth. After attending the first meeting, I could understand why such poor decisions were being made. The guys at the top were not getting facts, but fancy. Since torture wasn't working, I resolved to correct the situation.

Attendance at additional meetings were required, and I openly commenting whenever I heard a misstatement. Later, after I had answered my particular problem, I continued to attend the meetings, and to offer free advice to my management. To my delight and satisfaction, I observed that at least from my perspective, the quality of decisions issued from the Hot Seat meeting went way up, with fewer "bad" unilateral decisions being made.

I had discovered another great truth; **"It is easier to lead a horse by the nose than from the tail"!** In other words, if you have something important to say, then a way must be found to get the information into the hands of the powers that be before decisions occur. A decision once made is often very hard or impossible to undo.

From that time on, I considered it important for me to sit in on management reviews, because I felt that I had valuable insight to offer. Sit in I did. I was never ejected!

Process Setup Continues

John Dalton had begun to define and qualify the cleaning steps that could be used when tungsten was present. The presence of tungsten really complicated the cleaning steps, because tungsten dissolved in the reagents we normally used for bare silicon. Tungsten seemed to "want" to leap into the cleaning baths. We would also soon find that tungsten had the ability to react with small amounts of oxygen in process gasses, producing white powdery tungsten oxides. The chemical instability of tungsten was a severe problem, but we with chemical backgrounds felt that these problems could be managed. First, we had to get the tungsten to mechanically remain on the wafers.

Tungsten had two unique problems. First, the chemical bond between deposited films and the wafers was very weak. Second, the deposited films were in severe tension, and neither tungsten nor silicon is ductile. The films had an annoying habit of spontaneously falling or peeling off the wafers. Early on, exposing the deposited wafer to boiling water was the best adhesion test we had. If the film fell off into the beaker of boiling water, then the adhesion was bad. Hmmm. Sometimes the deposited films fell off directly after deposition. At other times, the film remained in place until circuit interconnections were formed by photolithography. Individual fine lines would then spontaneously simply curl up into what looked like very, very, very tiny clock springs after device patterns were etched. When these phenomena were repeatedly brought up in the daily meetings, Geoffrey would simply say something like; "You must have done something wrong! The tungsten did not just fall off!" Eventually we were able to deposit films with stress low enough that they did not spontaneously leap off our wafers. We also soon learned how to keep them from being converted into white powder in the high temperature steps. The adhesion matter would appear again at a training session for new supervisors. I'll have more to say about that later.

When test masks were available, Alan Moline and I immediately began to process short test sequences using the facility in 1E358 to better define the Phase 2 process details. Alan had prior experience with implanted source drains, and implanted gettering work, and we had the source-drain diode results from the Pickar-Dalton Picturephone^R target effort. In addition, we had the clean HCl oxides resulting from our earlier work, and knew that they could be used to determine the sources of any subsequent sodium contamination.

Sam began using the HCl oxides as a means of qualifying metal deposition techniques and systems for sodium contamination. The first tungsten to be certified as sodium-free was deposited by Bill Polito, using his electron-beam deposition system. Sam was then able to qualify all the relevant deposition equipment.

We also found many other problems, including "crud" forming on wafers resulting from implantation in

221

contaminating atmospheres, and we evaluated various high temperature steps containing small amounts of hydrogen that could anneal implant damage, while keeping tungsten from oxidizing away. More comprehensive masks became available and were processed in the Buckley Process Line (BPL), using the sequences we had previously worked out. Week after week, the effort ground on, and on, and on.

Training for New Bell Labs Supervisors

Phase 2 had been underway for some time when I was **required** to attend a training seminar for new Bell Labs supervisors. Attendance was mandatory, with no loopholes. Try as I would, I could find no way to avoid participation. (It was only much later that I discovered how to avoid these inconvenient exposures.) I believe that the seminar was held in a hotel located in Red Bank, New Jersey, not far from Holmdel, another major BTL Facility. The instructors were all BTL Employees, and included staff people as well as some department heads and higher, all people of note. Long-standing BTL technical management policy was to promote only those with excellent technical records, so the instructors would naturally include proven leaders, as well as professional training people.

As I recall, we arrived at the facility either on a Sunday night or early Monday morning, and left at midday Friday.

The facilities were plush, the food was good, and in the evenings, adult refreshments were served.

The sessions began with an outline of the work involved and we plunged immediately into the material. The professional trainers began with the presentation of some tools from psychology that were thought to be useful for us new recruits. One of the early concepts we were introduced to was the Johari Window describing the mutual state of awareness between an individual and others. The Johari Window is an x-y matrix of four panes. The two columns dealing with the state of self-awareness are labeled, "Known to Self", and "Unknown to Self". The two rows dealing with the awareness of others observing the individual are labeled "Known by Others", and "Unknown by Others". The ideas behind the Johari Window were not especially new, but the formalism of the matrix did facilitate understanding of interpersonal interactions. The objective of the discussion was to make us more aware of the two-way flow of information between individuals, presumably with an eye toward making us more capable supervisors. Since Bell Labs management was a strict meritocracy, we were only supposed to be more capable supervisors, not necessarily better people. The social revolution regarding women, worker's rights and minority problems were still relatively new in the workplace, and the ponderous BTL Intellectual Machine had barely focused on these issues.

I did get some reinforcement of some of my own earlier ideas from the Johari Window treatment. I had long before wondered what additional attributes might lie hidden within me. Here, in the lower right-hand quadrant, we were formally talking about the part of oneself that is hidden from one's own knowledge, where most of this unknown-to-self material is also unknown to others. In fact, it occurred to me that this quadrant was by far the largest part of our makeup.

The known parts were just glimpses of a great hidden mass, rather like the tips of huge icebergs of unknown and largely unreachable material. So when we said, **"I know that individual." what we meant was, "I know the little bit of that individual that is showing".** Further, **"If one cannot even know oneself, then how can it be said that we understand anyone else?"** When I asked this latter question, I got no real answer, and I expected none. Apparently, a meaningful answer was either inconvenient, or it was self-evident. The instructor had no useful response whatever. In my opinion, this question had been asked but remained unanswered since the boss-worker relationship first arose.

We participated in an exercise to illustrate how trivial, meaningless ideas can assume great importance. We were divided into four groups. Each of three groups was given a task to coin a slogan for the course, and the fourth group was to act as a "Supreme Court". After a set interval, the three groups were to meet in a forum to debate the merits of the three slogans, and hopefully to vote on a consensus. The Supreme Court was to rule if the popular vote was not two to one or three to none.

Each group had to pick a single representative to argue the merits of his case, and no one else was allowed to speak openly. Each Group Leader presented his slogan, among with a listing of the slogan's merits. After the first round of presentations, a vote was taken. As expected, each group voted for it's own slogan, so the situation was deadlocked. The floor was again thrown open for discussion, and again a vote was taken, with the same result. A third and final round of discussion followed, and it became apparent that the debaters and their followers had become partisans. Acrimony and hateful commentary became the norm. When the final vote was taken, one of the groups caved in and voted for another slogan, because they did not want the Supreme Court to make the decision. There was just no way of telling what that outcome would have been had the court picked the eventual winner.

In the end, after everyone calmed down, the presenters pointed out that in less than two hours, we had become passionately involved with the significance of a meaningless slogan. The assembled multitude had become angry, convinced of some imagined special quality of an obscure phrase. They pointed out that this was a facet of human nature often seen both in the workplace and in the world at large. I think of this example often when I watch political debates.

How Do We Effectively Communicate Upwards?

We spent several sessions on organizational structures and the advantages and disadvantages of the arrangements. The discussion was directed towards facilitating the downward flow of information, since it seemed that a new supervisor's major problem was to properly direct his troops in the field of our particular intellectual wars. After listening to this prattle for a while, I finally said, "We have spent some time dealing with how to communicate effectively with our troops. What do you have to say regarding how to communicate **up** the chain of command?" After some vaporware escaped the instructor's mouth, I was still not satisfied with his answer, as he switched back into his accustomed verbal track. **"Wait!"** I said, " I did not understand your answer! What do you do if you report something important to your boss, and your report is simply disregarded"? Again, an answer was given about "different perspectives", management prerogatives, and several other platitudinous non-answers, and again the instructor plunged on in his delivery.

"**WAIT!**" I said, "I still didn't understand your answer! Let me make the situation more specific, less theoretical. Let me set up a scenario. "**A wafer has just been handed to you following a photoshaping operation. My boss and I are looking at the wafer. Glancing at the wafer in reflected light, I think that I see something unusual, and put the wafer under a microscope to check on the wafer's appearance. Here and there, lines of circuit metallization are missing, and the surface is covered with little curled-up clock-springs.**" I say something like, "The metal is falling off!" and I invite my boss to look, and he says, "No the metal is not falling off, you must have done something wrong"! "Here then is the dilemma. I have tried to communicate **upward** with my boss concerning an apparently objective fact, and I have failed to succeed. What should I do?"

By this time, my fellow supervisors were sympathetic to the question, since many of them had faced similar situations, and they all wanted to hear a satisfactory answer.

227

There was no such response forthcoming. Finally, the annoyed instructor gave up trying and went on, ~~cleverly~~ simply avoiding the issue altogether.

There were to be two eventual outcomes of the upward communication question I had raised and then pressed for an answer, to no avail. The attendees were asked to come up with a phrase that best summarized the communication part of the course. The winner by a large margin was, "**The Metal IS Falling Off**"!

A second outcome after the conference occurred when I returned to Murray Hill on Friday afternoon directly following the training session. As I walked up a stairwell, by sheer chance I met Geoffrey Garrett coming down from the floors above. He remarked, "I understand that the metal is falling off. Is that so?" I said, "Yes indeed the metal falls off if you do it wrong!" We both smiled and parted with no apparent rancor. The incident was a bit bothersome, since the course principals had assured us that the matters discussed in the course were private, and would not go beyond the conference room walls. Apparently, the hotel walls extended many miles indeed. After all, the leadership had made a solemn privacy pledge, had they not?

In a little more than four days, the training session was over. I suppose that I might have thereby become a better supervisor but it was not obvious to me how. I had lost a week in what I thought to be critical times, and besides, the metal could still fall off, if things had been done wrongly.

I Discover and Capture a Stray ISI Scanning Electron Microscope

One day I was walking through the loading dock looking for an expected package, when I stumbled upon a wooden carton with large red lettering proclaiming, "Fragile – Delicate Electronic Equipment" and in smaller black letters, "ISI scanning Electron Microscope". The dock foreman told me it was being shipped back to ISI™. I took the shipping papers from him, and arranged to have it delivered to my old lab, where Bill Polito had his tungsten deposition station. Bill was really happy to receive the machine, and I instructed him to set it up and become proficient in its use, as I thought that we could use the machine to good purpose. He did, and we did. Al MacRae somehow protected me from the accountants, and we were able to keep the machine.

A goal of the Phase 2 effort was to produce random access memory technology that would be faster and less expensive than that of our competitors. Intel was selling memories in the 1025-kilobit range, and the largest memory in Western Electric production was only 256 bits, and was not designed to be compatible with Phase 2. Geoffrey had formed design groups led by Harry Boll to design the first test memory based on his original picture using rules that we had developed in our earlier exploratory processing programs.

H. J. (Harry) Boll

Philosophically and practically, we faced another problem. When we finished processing such devices, how could we easily separate process problems from design problems? I personally knew from my work with Hodges and Lepselter that debugging even simple circuits was sometimes difficult and complex, and for a large chip designed by a new team with new technology, the problem seemed really intractable, because it would take some time for Harry's team to do it's work. A short-term solution was formulated.

It was decided to make whatever modifications to the Allentown 256 bit memory design that were needed to make it compatible with Phase 2 processing. At least the 256-bit design was thought to work well, and testing routines were well developed. Geoffrey summoned a fairly well known person I will call Mr. Snort, and directed Mr. Snort to obtain the design, make the **absolute minimum** number of changes needed to make it compatible for our use. We confidently expected that masks would be available in perhaps a few weeks. After a while, Mr. Snort reported that new masks had been made, but inspection had shown that some feature had been put in an incorrect position, and the mask set was not useable. Each week, we would hear a similar story. The new masks would again unusable. We would shake our heads in disbelief, and after each meeting, Geoffrey would ask, "What is wrong with that man"?

The *Cat Pee Syndrome* is Named

I had a male cat named Fu Manchu that my family had adopted when he was a small kitten. This black and white cat had magnificent white whiskers, was friendly and a fierce fighter, seldom losing battles with other tomcats. He had only one persistent fault. He had a tendency to decorate the interior of our house with his urine. What an odor! No amount of punishment seemed to make any difference. He was largely banished from the house, depriving both him and me each other's company.

One day while meditating in my Supercoupe on the way to work, I understood the connections between these two types of events, and at the earliest opportunity, told Garrett of my insight. "We are observing an example of what I will call the **Cat Pee Syndrome.**" I said, and explained the problem by referring to my cat Fu Manchu. "Fu Manchu pees on things around him because that is how he marks his territory. **He has to pee** to know that he has been there." If I want to stop this behavior, I have only three choices. I can exclude him from my presence or kill him, but both courses seem self-defeating. I could castrate him, but at this stage, that solution probably won't work either. I could also give him away and thereby give the problem to someone else".

I continued, "Mr. Snort is a highly trained intelligent man. We have asked him to do a menial job. His intellect forces him to make unnecessary changes. Only in that way can he make a contribution meaningful to himself. Mr. Snort is suffering from the **Cat Pee Syndrome**!" Garrett looked at me strangely, shook his head slowly, and indicated that he might even agree me, but I could not be sure. We <u>never</u> got a satisfactory mask set from all this effort, and I am reasonably certain that I had correctly diagnosed the problem.

There is a corollary conclusion to be drawn about the **Cat Pee Syndrome**. If you want a repetitive menial task to be preformed reliably, do not use a hyperactive mind. The hyperactive mind will have a great deal of trouble doing such tasks repeatedly. If you force such an individual to do so, there is a good chance that you will kill his mind. What then will you have gained?

Memory Chip Masks Available, My Activities Split

Harry Boll and his troops finished the design of a one-kilobit memory chip. We had completed our initial process studies in 1E358, and Rusty's BPL began running memory device lots.

The role of my group split into two distinct functions. In the processing arena, we began to use 1E358 to develop the last part of the process for devices completed by the BPL. I think that from the beginning, the plan was to put beam leads on wafers that survived past functional testing. Pete Byrnes and I had looked at tests run on dummy wafers prior to submitting Phase 2 devices to the standard beam lead sequence. We discovered that a thin diaphanous film often remained after the platinum and titanium removal steps, and that the residual film was conductive. We showed that spray etching with an added surfactant completely removed the offending film. A patent case was written up for the etching technique, but the effort to patent was eventually abandoned. Thus, the discovery became part of the "art" instead of patented intellectual property.

Miles Sullivan was assigned to 1E358 as the resident lithographer. Miles Sullivan was the inventor of the "dunking woodpecker" then sold throughout the U. S. Miles was a mild mannered <u>expert</u> PhD chemist, but he seemed to take the assignment well. It was his fate to serve as lithographic technician for an indefinite time. I thought about the **Cat Pee Syndrome**, but did not try to block the assignment. To Miles' credit, he did not crack, and eventually escaped unharmed, at least as far as I could tell.

As devices began to come out of the BPL, they would be functionally tested. Sam began to look at the non-functional devices, and where device failure could be traced to a particular location, he could infer at least some failure modes by looking at the electrical characteristics, somewhat in the same way that he had done on the AIM phototransistor arrays somewhat earlier. When he found defects that he thought he could identify, we would think through the possible origins of the defect. Bill Polito became proficient using his little ISI SEM, and was able to identify at least some of the physical defects that caused the electrical fault. Eventually we were able to develop a catalogue of failures, and using 1E358, were able to recommend further mask and process changes to enable non-zero device yields.

Next target, World's Largest CCD Devices

Results were beginning to be encouraging, and Garrett wanted to build a device that would make a huge public relations impact. It was decided to build the world's largest CCD[14] arrays. The CCD device was a fundamentally simple device as envisioned by the CCD inventors, W. S. Boyle and G. Smith, both BTL contemporaries. The very long CCD device was designed and masks generated. The CCD's required over 135 field-butted master reticules for the masks, an all-time record, and a dubious honor. The CCD arrays stretched over almost the entire width of a wafer, so only a few could be accommodated. Projection wafer printers had just become available, and Buckley had an early version made by Tamarak.

The imaging devices were indeed spectacular in appearance, with each wafer only able to accommodate around twenty complete devices. This was long before the large imaging arrays of today became routine to make. A poor photograph of one of the wafers from the BPL is shown on the next page:

---

[14] W. S Boyle and G. E. Smith invented the CCD, and in 2009, received a Nobel Prize for their efforts.

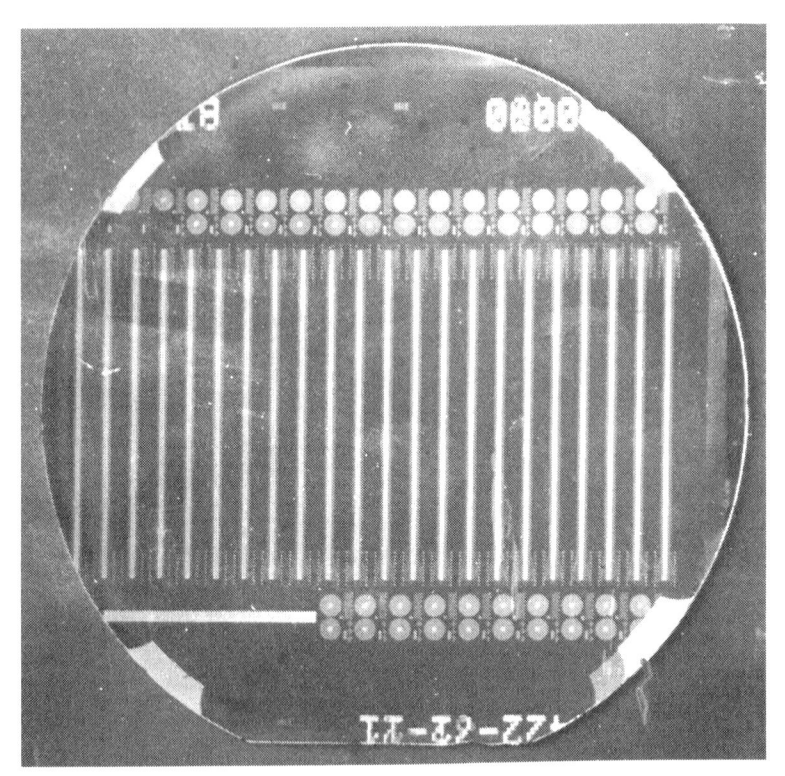

22 Phase 2 CCDs Fabricated on 2 in Wafer by BPL

CCD wafers began to come out of the BPL, initially with very low yields, but after a while, data fed into the front of some CCD's began to make it all the way to the output pin. Such wafers would be then given to us in 1E358, and we would put beam leads on them for eventual final assembly. The results of our efforts would be expected at the Monday morning (soon to be in mourning) hot spot inquisition.

A Super Wafer is Fabricated! OOPS! ***Superwafer Dies****!!*

Eventually, a CCD wafer appeared with really good properties. More careful testing showed that at least one of the devices had all-time record electrical properties. It was designated **"Super Wafer"**. **Super Wafer** was passed on to us for beam lead processing late on a Friday afternoon. We were used to working late and continued processing that evening. The wafer was coated with titanium-palladium, and Miles Sullivan loaded the wafer into our resist spinner, as needed for the then-standard process then used to define the beam lead pattern. Unfortunately, the spinner lost vacuum while merrily doing its usually routine job, thereby dropping super **wafer** into an exposed internal metal turbine. When the machine stopped spinning, we opened the lid, and observed a whole lot of tiny pieces of shiny silicon, surely thousands of tiny, tiny bits. Our spinner had converted the record-breaking **Super Wafer** into silicon dust!

Our hearts momentarily stopped beating, then we went through periods of intense sweating and cold shivers. We wondered if Pitcairn Island had any semiconductor equipment, or where we might find another means of making a living. I think that I called Al MacRae immediately. I figured that his weekend might as well be ruined as well as mine.

As I drove toward home in Allentown, I had time to consider my options. Suicide seemed too extreme, and further lateral transfer was not a likely out. The English Mafia would seek me out wherever I tried to go in the system. I arrived home without having resolved my quandary. I told Judy about my misadventure, and even after a lot of scotch whiskey, things did not seem brighter. I had what remained of the weekend to consider my course of action. I think that I was even poorer company than usual.

Eventually I remembered what my Dad said he had done when in the late 1920's he could not make car payments. Dad had walked up the stairs to the loan officer, saying, "I can't make the payment this month". The Loan Officer asked him where the car was, and Dad replied, "The car is downstairs." and put the car keys on the desk. The loan officer looked at him carefully, and gave him back the keys saying, "Make the payment when you can". Dad considered that honesty, confronting such problems directly and in person, was the best policy. I knew that I would have to take this tack.

Monday morning arrived. The commute from Allentown to Murray Hill seemed to take an inordinate, if somehow not quite enough, time. The Monday morning meeting began, and I sat next to Al. When it was my turn to report, I stood up, walked over to Garret and David Thomas, and handed them a glass petri dish containing at least some of the **Super Wafer** dust. Wide eyes looked at the Glittering Bits and Initial Disbelief greeted my grim news. Assorted murmuring, grumbles, groans, and gasps could be heard throughout the room. Both Garrett and Thomas turned various shades of red and white. Al stood up and said something like, "It's not Tag's fault! The resist machine ate the wafer! Tag was just unlucky!" After a short pause, Geoffrey replied, **"I like lucky people!"** I do not recall the rest of the meeting. After the meeting, further analysis revealed a design flaw in the commercial spinner that made the machine potentially unreliable. I beat the damn machine into a twisted mass of metal with a sledgehammer. For some reason, Miles Sullivan, the actual operator of the spinner escaped entirely without notice. I guess that I must have deflected the heat and fury.

1E358   ->->->->->   "Crash Pad"

From that day forward, my facility was referred to as "**Crash Pad**". I think that this incident cost me at least half of any potential annual raise, maybe more, regardless of any other accomplishments. The loss would turn out to be at least partially offset by an interesting quirk of fate. At the next joint merit review with Allentown people, the exploits of Pete Panousis were being extolled by Jim Goldey, his director, explaining how Pete had solved the Si_3N_4 problem, saving the company untold losses of revenue. Garrett let him talk on, like a fisherman landing a prize fish, and when Goldey's presentation was finished, the value of Pete's effort was clearly established to **all**. Garret then quietly pointed out in his best-measured British accent that I was co-inventor of the fix, and so I deserved equal credit. Thus, I was saved at least some fraction, perhaps all, of what I lost in the catastrophic death of our star **Superwafer**.

I am not certain exactly how it came about, but I developed an alternative method for forming beam leads featuring electroless gold, thereby sidestepping several tedious, but routine process steps. Y. Okinaka, a BTL electrochemist, had invented a new electroless gold deposition bath. Okinaka's gold deposition process required no electrical contact and resulted in high quality pure gold deposits. The electroless process deposited gold by a locally catalyzed reaction, needing only an exposed metal surface to start the chemistry. Dick Sard, another electrochemist, was assigned to help in application of this technology to Phase 2 devices.

R. (Dick) Sard

If we were to use this electroless gold technique, we still needed to know to how to simply form the beam lead pattern on the wafers. Otherwise, the standard beam lead process of the day using photoresist to mask the beam lead plating pattern would have to be used. I previously had read about very early use of shadow masks and the more modern lift-off techniques. It occurred to me that we might utilize a variant of this old technique to form our beam leads without using photoresist.

I invented a very advanced shadow mask holder for our purpose. As the name implies, a shadow mask is a thin metal membrane with holes in it that is placed between an evaporation source and a substrate, so that deposition on the substrate occurs only through the openings on the mask. This assumes that the shadow mask is in close proximity to the substrate and is aligned correctly, both difficult problems.

241

I created a nifty and unique shadow mask holder that had three functions. First, It held the shadow mask in a precision upper frame made of the weakly ferromagnetic material, nickel. Second, a disk magnet, ground to be extremely flat and with a uniform thickness, sat on the nickel fixture base, and formed the surface upon which the wafer rested. When the nickel frame/associated shadow mask and disc magnet were brought into contact, they were held snugly together by a moderate magnetic force, with the wafer gently trapped in between the disk magnet and shadow mask. The gap between the magnetic disc and the shadow mask was chosen so that the wafer was captured and restrained in a fixed relative position when the frame and disc magnet were placed in contact.

The entire assembly was designed to fit into our standard wafer alignment system. For alignment, vacuum was applied to the bottom of the wafer using the standard wafer chuck by means of holes drilled through the magnetic disc. The upper part of the shadow mask frame was grasped and held by the separate vacuum chuck which normally held the mask in our standard mask aligner, thereby enabling separation of the shadow mask and wafer/base so that alignment could be accomplished without rubbing contact between the shadow mask and wafer. Following alignment, the assembly was again brought into contact, and the magnetic force held everything in precise alignment, so that either titanium-palladium or titanium-platinum could be subsequently vacuum-deposited. The deposited metals formed the base patterns for eventual electroless gold plating.

Shadow Mask Assembly Used to Deposit TI/Pd Pattern
for Phase 2 Beam Leaded Devices

The shadow mask system worked like a charm, as did the electroless gold process. This combination was used for all further beam lead formation of Phase 2 devices. A patent study for the holder was initiated, and eventually the shadow mask technique was bundled with an umbrella patent for the final Phase 2 structure. The electroless gold beam lead process became routine, and no further wafers were lost. I could now concentrate on the BPL process problems.

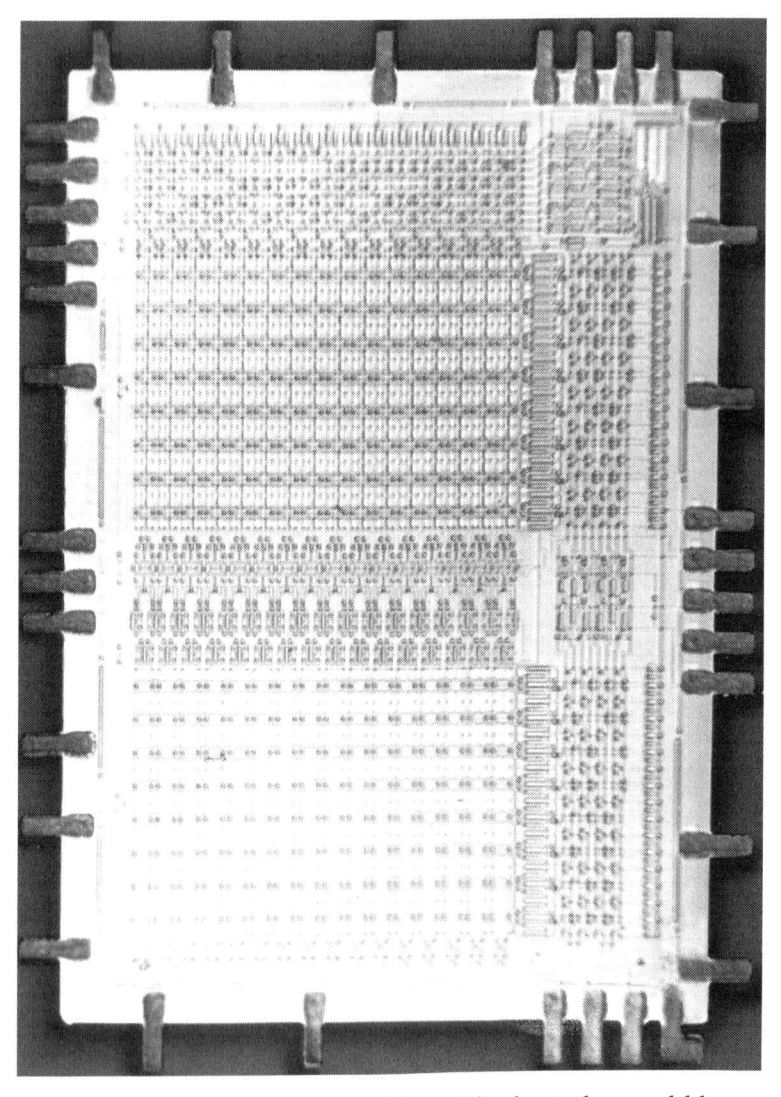

One kilobit Phase 2 memory chip with electroless gold beam Leads.

Sam Broydo and I Continue to Analyze Phase 2 Devices.

The wafer start rate in Rusty Buckley's BPL was steadily increasing. Garret and Thomas believed that only by running very hard could the "real" problems be revealed. It seemed to me that they were pushing the problem with a limp noodle, but the English Mafia leaders could not be persuaded to relent. Their instruction manual, probably acquired in an advanced managerial training course, bade them to press ever onward. Wafer lots would come out, parametric electrical measurements made, and then functional tests performed on wafers that appeared to possess the proper parameters. Early yields were fair. Friction soon developed between Buckley and me, similar to that between Murray Hill and Allentown. Sam and I had the luxury of thinking about what was happening, whereas Rusty was saddled with orders that required marching onward, regardless of all odds or difficulties. Cooperation became limited. Garret and Thomas were mercilessly whipping Rusty on and he perceived us as needlessly sticking sharp sticks into his sides. Getting wafer data for meaningful analysis became a real problem.

All test data gathered by Rusty was kept in the vestibule of his facility, which he soon declared out of bounds to personnel not reporting directly to him. We needed the data but could not gain access to it. We did not want to be content with the executive summaries that he routinely supplied at the daily meetings. We employed a subterfuge. We hired a cute female clerk, Steffie Graff, to transcribe the data. She charmed Mr. Buckley, and thereafter transcribed the data for us unimpeded. Rusty was happy, Sam and I were happy, and the additional data gave us a much better handle on the situation inside the facility.

S. Graff

It soon becoming apparent that although the rate of wafer starts was steadily rising as Garrett and Thomas desired, more and more of the wafers were dead when they reached test. Sam prepared a plot showing wafer yield vs. time. The plot showed that the overall yield would go to **zero** within two months. When the plot was presented at the daily meeting, it was if we had exploded a grenade in the room. The Pall was at least equivalent to that generated by the death of Superwafer. When the smoke cleared, I commented that the technical people associated with the facility were overwhelmed and numb. Fresh new eyes and firm hands were needed to rescue the situation. **I proposed that I take temporary responsibility for the line, with full authority and responsibility for all the activities therein.**

To my slight surprise, my offer was accepted over the sputtering, repeated objections of Mr. Buckley. His lamentations mattered little to me. I was not running in a popularity contest. We were fighting for the survival of a semiconductor effort in the Bell System. The specter of RCA making all the Bell System devices was looming just outside the field of view in my rear view mirror!

We Take Command of the BPL – Both Shifts!

I asked for the addition of Mike Grieco to my team. Mike was a man with a lot of energy and experience in photolithography, one of the central problem areas in the facility. Sam, Mike, and I took charge of the BPL almost immediately. We were to bridge both shifts for several months. It was to be an exhausting, sobering time, and one of the more successful endeavors of my whole Phase 2 experience.

We were issued cleanroom garments, and leaving Buckley outside, we at last entered the inner sanctum of the BPL facility. The first order of the day was to clear the facility of what we called the walking dead. I sent the operating personnel away for Buckley to take care of in some responsible manner. We started to visually inspect wafers under microscopes, starting with the oldest lots first. We found that lot after lot needed to be discarded due to one major problem or another. We filled the trash containers with useless wafers. We kept meticulous records as to what was discarded and what we found. The facility had been working two shifts, and I think that we worked both shifts that day. When we finished the second shift of the second day we were really, really tired, and there were a whole lot fewer wafers within the facility waiting further processing.

On the third day, we seemed to be finding much fewer lots to throw away. This bothered me, and at lunch, I realized what was happening. <u>We were beginning to see what we wanted to see instead of what was actually there</u>, and were passing on junk wafers! In this very short time, we had succumbed to the same malady that claimed the usual facility technical personnel. In a sense, we had succumbed to the **Cat Pee Syndrome**. We were too highly trained to continue long in such a tedious job. Our minds had simply turned off and **we all three of us had suddenly lost objectivity**. I shared my insight with Sam and Mike, and said that we needed to change our strategy. Immediately!

We put together some picture posters illustrating what to look for, and brought the inspection people back into the facility to do the inspections for us. They had no axe to grind, and as I expected, they could work steadily, well, and without bias. Thus, the inspection rate went up, the rejection rate went back up, and we could now spend time thinking about solutions to the problems that were found. This variant of the **Cat Pee Syndrome** had <u>almost</u> defeated us!

The Brushes are a Problem – We Use Water Spray

The main problems we found were of two kinds. Poor lithography and the subtler problem of debris left in the bottom of inter-level contact holes. We tackled the debris problem first. The debris was identified as bits of white powder, oxidized remnants of tungsten resulting from extraneous holes in the overlying dielectric during a high temperature step, as well as bits of material from the brushes used in the cleaning step. One of the cleaning steps that had been developed for Picturephone was the use of a rotating brush to remove stubbornly adherent particles. This type of clean **<u>had been essential</u>** for the very flat Picturephone targets, but was of little use here. The brush was sweeping particles off the outer surface, but was depositing many particles in low regions, such as contact windows. These particles would contaminate the next step, and the degradation was cumulative. We found that the brush clean had to be abandoned.

I had recent experience with spray etching techniques when removing titanium residues, and found that high-pressure spraying with pure water would totally eliminate the particles from all regions. A simple sweep with high-pressure pure water spray, and the particles were totally gone! It was like magic! We cautiously applied the spray technique to some lots near completion and were pleased to find that cosmetically, they looked great! Our elation was short lived. When the test results came in, the yields were even lower than before. Worse, the few "good" devices were not reliable. It didn't take us long to understand the problem, and I again shut the line down. Our opponents were salivating in their lairs, awaiting the opportunity to discredit us, or worse.

We realized that the high-pressure high-purity water was generating static electricity, and we were blowing out the gate oxides! Rusty could hardly contain himself. We had been bold and offensive, now **we** surely would be vanquished and shamed! We were not to be defeated so easily. As in the past, I knew that it was not a time for timidity. If our will and intelligence did not desert us, we would be successful.

High Pressure Pure Water Spray = Static Generator

The water spray was acting as a static electricity generator, like a comb running through your hair on a dry day. In effect, the pure water spray made a small Van De Graff generator. A similar phenomenon causes lightning in thunderstorms. The answer to the problem was simple. Make the water slightly conducting! Making the water conducting would not allow charge buildup and the static electricity problem would vanish. Adding a little ammonia to the water solved the problem completely. Ammonia was chosen to "de-purify" the water because it was completely volatile and would leave no residue on the wafers. Rusty and other detractors could only watch from the sidelines, as we not only survived, we grew in competence in the face of severe adversity. As I had predicted, neither our courage nor our wits failed us. We could not be easily unhorsed.

We reactivated the line, now equipped with the new spray clean, and the first lots completed gave much better test results, and reliability tests improved. We now had only the photolithography problem to solve. I turned my complete attention to understanding this problem.

The Lithography Solution – Improve Control and Minimize Changes

Mike Grieco was my lithography expert, and had been working in the field for a number of years. Mike was short and stocky, but except for his size, he attacked photolithography with the gusto of an Errol Flynn.

Photolithography was unlike any of the other processing steps. The lithographer could coat a test wafer with a resist film, bake, expose, and develop it in around a half hour. Visual inspection of the result than gave almost real-time feedback. It was feasible to easily perform several such test cycles, if needed, to "zero in" the process. Once the process was zeroed in, the test wafer could rejoin the lot, and processing of the lot could proceed. There was also exposure, post-bake and other variables that could be adjusted if needed. Since there were a number of wafer lots in the facility all at different steps, the situation was hectic. No, the situation was chaotic but exciting. I came to understand that successful lithographers all had personalities that thrived on this chaos. As I had previously found with such individuals, they all tended to be swashbucklers. Some simply swashed and buckled better than others.

As I watched the process, Mike would apply resist to a lot (group) of wafers, put one wafer from the lot into a petri dish for his experimentation. Next he would bake the wafer in its dish for some set time and either inspect it visually or go through the rest of the steps to decide if the printing was satisfactory. If the test wafer looked good, then the lot would be committed to the process. Our inspection people would then report the result of their own visual inspection. Unfortunately, the inspection results were mixed, and often relatively poor. Days went by with few positive results. Rusty would occasionally stop by the facility outer window, gently shake his head, and smile slightly, enjoying our obvious discomfort, while fretting over his facility, and perhaps his future.

Massive Aluminum Oven Walls and Simplified Control Practices

One evening while sleeping at home, I awoke and I realized what the problem was. The facility was using a flimsy thin-walled oven to bake the wafers prior to exposure. The petri dish containing the test wafer sat on a thin metal shelf, and the cassettes carrying the full wafer lots were simply placed into the oven for an equal amount of time. The little oven could not possibly be said to have a specific temperature, nor could it be said that wafers all had equivalent bake conditions. Any cook knows that opening the oven door changes baking times, and that the front, back, top, and bottom of the oven behave differently. What we needed was a better baking system that would allow better definition of the cooking schedules.

That morning, I called in and left a message for the facility to be immediately shut down once more. **No** further processing was to take place! I called the foreman of the Murray Hill machine shop, and left a message, "We have a line down, and I urgently need your help. Stand by!" When I got to work, I sketched up an oven modification to alleviate the problem. I arranged for an oven insert to be made of one and one half inch thick aluminum plates that formed four massive aluminum tunnels. The tunnels were sized to comfortably hold a single wafer cassette each, with a lot of room at each end. Within hours, the insert was delivered, cleaned, and placed in the oven. It just fit, as designed. It took several hours to get the insert temperature up to the desired value. Now we could be much more confident that the oven would have a very uniform temperature, regardless of how many times the door was opened.

Mike began recalibrating the exposures, now with a better defined baking setup In addition, we decided that from then on, any test wafer would only be taken from a lot that was baked as a unit, and the test wafers would be momentarily set aside for later processing, so that the balance of the lot would experience as uniform processing as possible. When enough of the test wafers had been accumulated, the group so collected would continue processing, identified by a new lot number.

The results were dramatic! Inspection results were impressive, the throughput went up, and the yields jumped. We still had fine-tuning to do, but we had made it over the hump. The line was not only stabilized, it was operating with higher throughput, and with wafers having much higher yield. We had one additional task to perform. Sam and I wrote out a streamlined process flow that eliminated a few adjectives, and we started processing lots using this new simplified sequence. There were far fewer steps involved, so process time was reduced, and the number of lots that could be processed went up. The yields again took a step up. I don't recall that Garret noticed that we had eliminated a few of his adjectives, but if he did, he did not stop us.

Superwafer Wounds are Healed, With Little Scarring

By this time, all the shrapnel wounds in my body had healed, and I had mentally recovered from the horrendous death of Superwafer. The line was running smoothly and achieving pretty high memory yields. Passant Chawla had been given the charter to develop a test chip full of specialized

255

structures intended to better determine the process sensitivities of our technology. This chip became known the Chawla Chip, and when masks were available, the line began to fill up with lots composed of test structures. As we ramped up the number of test structures, the number of actual device structures would soon be zero. After the first few Chawla lots were processed, it quickly became apparent to us that there was no useful data to be gained. The reason for the lack of useful data was simple. All of the test structures quickly yielded 100%! The Chawla Chip was not complex enough to find any defects!

I had expressed the concern that the operators and engineers alike knew that these were only test wafers, and because we had already solved the problems they were designed to test, they were only busy work. I was concerned that minimum effort would necessarily result, because everyone in the facility knew that his or her efforts were to little purpose. Garrett did not buy my point of view, and I uncharacteristically bit my tongue and bided my time.

At one of the **hot spot** meetings with Garret and Thomas present, I could refrain myself no longer. I asked. **"When are we going to make something worthwhile? We are processing toys! If I wanted to make toys, I would have gone to work for Mattel!"** Thomas coolly replied, "I do not think that the people care what they process, they will do as they are asked". The experience with Jim Early had shown me that being right was of little value when you have to challenge upper management to a duel. I promptly pointed out that it was time for the facility to be returned to Buckley. I didn't think that Rusty would care what they were running.

Some time after that **hot spot** meeting, we reluctantly (heh-heh!) relinquished control of the BPL back to Rusty. There was still work to be done, but we did not need to run the facility to do it. The Twin Tomcats, Sam and Tag, had to get away from the unending pressure of the facility or we would suffer brain death. Working for Rusty was not our cup of tea. I think that Rusty kept control of Mike for a time. Such was the price of battle.

We Study Putting Beam Leads on Aluminum

It became evident to many of us that the second level of tungsten we were developing could well be replaced by aluminum. Aluminum was the industry-standard second level metallization, and while not capable of withstanding high temperatures, aluminum was chemically more stable than tungsten. The Bell System had committed to beam leads for the chip interconnect, so that I felt it would be useful to learn how to put gold beam leads on wafers with second level aluminum metal. In order to keep a low profile, I advised my people to make this a "dirty bell jar" effort, and to limit discussions with people outside our group, a sort of "secret" project. Keeping a low profile would possibly help us avoid low flying arrows. We began defining conditions for forming such leads, and looking at their long-term stability.

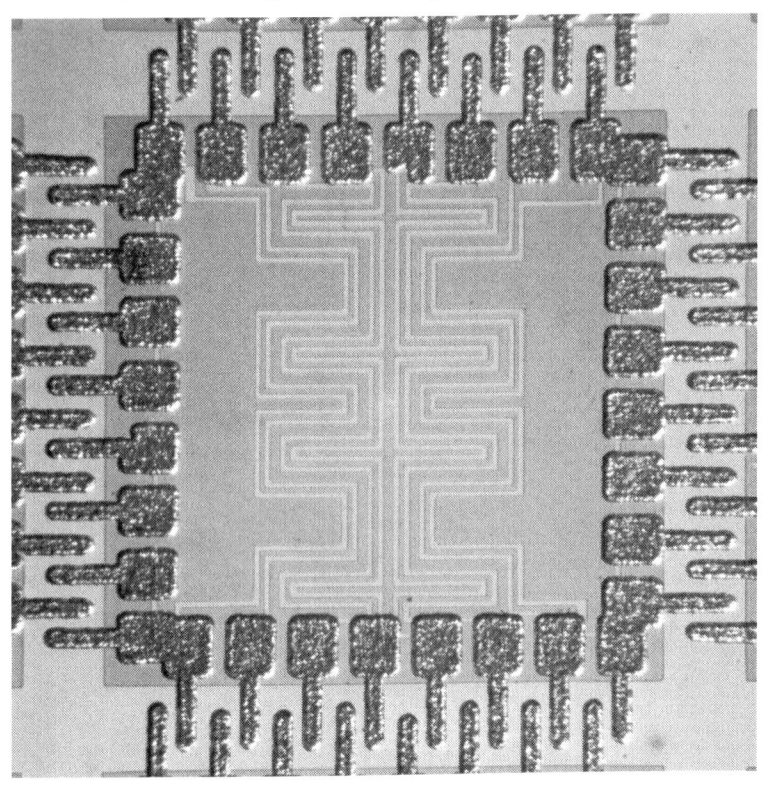

Test chip for measuring the interfacial aging of beam leads when applied to aluminum metallization.

More Corvair Tales

During this time, I had driven two Corvairs, first a black 1964 2-door Supercoupe, and now my canary yellow

1966 4-door sedan. They had both served me well. The Supercoupe had demonstrated an uncanny ability to move forward on everything except glare ice and deep show. I had two opportunities to experience driving on glare ice. The first occasion occurred only a few blocks from home, when I discovered that I could not get up the hill only a few blocks from my home, since freezing rain had converted the roads into sheets of black ice. I carefully returned home, and spent the day in Allentown. The second occasion occurred when I was about a third of the way to work. The day was cold and misty, but I had no trouble leaving Allentown, and even though the road was wet, passed uneventfully through Easton, Pennsylvania. The roadway in adjoining Phillipsburg New Jersey also presented no problem, but leaving the town, traffic began to slow.

Highway 22 takes a few turns just east of town and as I rounded a sharp right corner, I found all the cars in the ditches, and a jackknifed semi blocking the way. I had previously slowed and carefully came to a stop, but the stop did not last long. As I sat quietly in the car, it slowly accelerated and slid into the loose gravel next to the highway before coming to rest. After a while, the roadway ice melted, the truck was removed, and my journey to Murray Hill completed. I had lived to drive another day. I would experience only minor driving incidents, until my involvement in a multi-car pileup on route 22 just east of Bethlehem.

I was driving in normal rush-hour traffic headed east on highway 22. The highway was crowded, and both lanes of eastbound traffic were moving at around 70 mph, quite normal for the conditions. I was driving in the left hand lane, and following my usual practice, had left some considerable distance between the car in front and me. To my horror, I observed a flatbed semi pull into the left hand lane in such a way as to run his left rear dual tires up onto the trunk of the car in front of me! The rear of the car was pushed into the pavement causing a large shower of sparks that flew over both lanes of the roadway.

As I began braking, the truck driver realized what he had done and steered his truck off the fellow's trunk. Unfortunately, the driver of the injured car put on his brakes, and decided to come to a stop, sitting squarely in the center of my lane. I was able to stop safely without hitting anything (trusty Corvair), but looking in my rear view mirror, I could see cars behind me sliding in wild disarray, and even more spectacularly, saw a large truck rising up on top of the cars behind, all headed in my general direction! It was only a matter of seconds before the melee reached me!

I began weaving past the car in front of me and almost escaped unharmed, when I was gently clipped by a sliding pickup truck before I was able to move out of harm's way and park. When the sound of breaking machines ceased, I grabbed my clipboard, and walked back to the accident scene to record license plate numbers, names of witnesses, and other relevant information.

The accident had occurred on a bridge over the Lehigh River, and the cab of the large looming truck was now hanging over the riverbed, with the back end of the truck mating with various other mashed-up vehicles. The two passengers in the truck not only had an exciting ride, but also were now facing the possibility of falling into the river, some 70 feet below. I don't know how many vehicles were involved, but felt lucky to have escaped with so little damage. I turned over my writings to the state police when they finally arrived. It would turn out that no one was killed, and my recorded table of events notwithstanding, the driver of the truck was not even reprimanded by the authorities. I would later wonder who was paying what and to whom.

I never got the damage to my right fender repaired, because I simply didn't want to take the time. I would continue to drive the car for several years. I drove the car with son John, and cat Fu Manchu, to Illinois in a snowstorm in

1973. The snow was not a problem, but a terrified tomcat[15] cat was. I continued to assure my son John, "**The Corvair could not be stopped!**" **It wasn't!** I now return to my commuting days in an earlier time.

My Corvair was to figure large in another way. I had begun smoking as a senior in college, and the nicotine habit had latched onto my mental and physical apparatus to the tune of two and one half pack of Kent™ cigarettes/day. Like almost all smokers, I had "quit" many times, but to no avail. Within hours to days, I would be smoking again. I was finally able to cease smoking "forever". In preparation for the attempt, I had bought a package of **Stimudents™** to satisfy my oral aggressions as I stopped smoking.

STIM·U·DENT.
PLAQUE REMOVERS
MINT FLAVOR
FIGHTS GUM DISEASE
Contents: 25
Johnson&Johnson

One evening just before bed, I took my **last** cigarette a few hours before going to sleep, saying to myself, "I can make

---

[15] Fu Manchu provided the experimental evidence for my recognition and naming of "**The Cat Pee Syndrome**", discussed earlier.

it until morning". The next morning, I grabbed a Stimudent, and told myself that I could make it into my car. As I got into my car, I told myself, "I can make it to Easton". When Easton and its service stations were safely past, I got another Stimudent and told myself, "I can make it to Murray Hill". When I got to Murray Hill I told myself, "I can make it to Lunch", etc. Thus, using a copious number of Stimudents and very short-term goals, I was able to cease[16] smoking. The commute was a critical part of the withdrawal, because once in the car, I was relatively insulated from temptation. The sight of me with a Stimudent in my mouth became routine at Bell. Joe Ligenza gave me a giant framed version for my promotion party, and in the future, I would enter Teletype Corporation with a Stimudent in my mouth.

I have continued to use Stimudents up to this day, now only to keep my gums healthy, not to keep from smoking. I think that I am still addicted to cigarettes, but I have not had a single cigarette in the intervening forty or so years.

---

[16] Once an addict, always an addict.

Chapter 7 – Phase 2 Declared a Success

With the success of the BPL operation, Phase two was officially declared a success. We celebrated and gladly retired from the field of this particular battle. The Phase 2 mobilization involved many more groups and important individuals that I have not described in this narrative. Many of these people played vital roles necessary for success of the program. To set the scale, the grapevine reported that Phase 2 had cost around 50 million dollars, but I have no way of knowing if the number had any basis in reality. When success was declared, we were soon to be again reorganized.

Two Samari Present Talks at ECS, Miami FL

The success of the BPL meant that Sam and I could now be given time to decompress. We had been in a pressure cooker not of our making, and we wanted some time for repair. Not only that, the need and relevance of the weekly

'Hot Seat" meetings had diminished. We proposed that we take the opportunity to present two talks at an upcoming Electrochemical Society meeting. The first paper was "Growth Properties and Applications of High Temperature HCL-O2 Oxides" by S. Broydo, J. V. Dalton, W. J. Polito, and H. A. Waggener. The abstract is reproduced below:

> An oxidation system, where Si is oxidized in a dry O_2-HCl gas mixture, is described. The oxidation is followed by an inert gas anneal. The oxides were used to produce SiO_2-Si structures with mobile charge $<2 \times 10^{10}$ ch/cm^2. The properties of W-SiO_2-Si MOS devices were studied in detail. Bulk lifetimes of 100-300μsec, surface recombination velocities of 0.08-0.12 cm/sec, have been observed. Values of N_{ss} and Q_{ss} have been measured to be typically 5×10^{10}/cm^2/eV and $\sim 10^{10}$ ch/cm^2 respectively. V_{FB} was found to be .5 v more positive than in other thermally grown oxides. However, it was established that this anomaly is not due to the negative Q_{ss}. The oxides proved to be of good device quality and are currently being used in LSI.

I presented the second paper, "Control of Silicon Etch Rates in Hot Alkaline KOH Solutions by Externally Applied Potentials" by Herbert A. Waggener. This abstract is reproduced on the following page:

```
Hot alkaline solutions have found extensive use in the
etching of slots in air and dielectric isolated integrated
circuits. In such applications, the etch rates in the (100),
(110) and (111) directions determine wall geometry. Precise
control (±5%) of the (100) and (110) etch rates has been
achieved by controlling the silicon-solution potential during
separation/isolation etching. 4.55N KOH:H₂O solutions sat-
urated with either n propanol or sec butanol have been
studied at 80°C. Over a suitable voltage range, the (100)
and (110) etch rates R, depend linearly upon the potential,
v,:   R = a+bv. The constants a and b depend upon the crystal
face and the specific alcohol. It has been shown that
etching defect density decreases as the silicon potential
becomes more positive.
```

There might have been some <u>other</u> earth-shaking talks at this meeting, but I paid little if any attention. The beaches had just been reconstructed at great public expense, and stretched as far as the eye could see up and down the coast. Sam and I naturally spent some time on the beach, relaxing, talking, and observing the girls.

Samari Warriors

As we talked, we mused about our experience we had just lived through in Phase 2. Sam noted the similarity to the plot in "The Seven Samari", or even closer, the book, "Day of The Jackal". In times of great need, the toughest, most able fighters are brought in, and they can demand and get whatever is needed to solve the problem. They can demand almost anything, because there is little choice. However, once the problem is resolved, the prime fighters are no longer needed. In fact, it is necessary for them to recede into the background, so that life can go on as usual.

We were such men. We had been called in, we demanded much, received a few wounds, solved the problems, and now were no longer of great importance. Such was the role of the Samari. The girls on the beach still looked good to us. I don't recall having a bad sunburn upon leaving the meeting, but I don't know why not.

There was a second phenomenon that bothered us. We had been told that the company's future was at stake, and we felt that we had reacted accordingly. However, we had also noted that upper management still seemed to be keeping normal office hours. Where were their swords when things were so desperate? I don't think that we came to a useful conclusion on this latter matter, but for my own part, I suspected the worst.

When Phase 2 ended, we were awash in memory chips that nobody in the system wanted. More importantly, we were to be reorganized and realigned to work on new tasks. We would not return to work on bipolar devices of any kind in order to continue our massed talent concentration on Insulated

Gate Field Effect Transistor (IGFET) technology, also known in the industry as MOS or metal oxide and semiconductor devices. As was standard practice, members of BTL had invented this technology but the organization had failed to implement it well in production devices. The self-aligned load transistor that Dawan Kahng had patented in 1963, and the self-aligned silicon gate transistor patented by R. E. Kerwin, D. L. Klein, and J. C. Sarace in 1967 were the basis for much of the industry that threatened to make us current Bell Labs semiconductor technology purveyors totally irrelevant.

Dawan Kahng

R. (Bob) Kerwin

A Management Change – Phil Boddy Takes Over – April 1973

My first Department Head, Eric Iwersen, became Director of the new Unipolar Integrated Circuit Laboratory. Reporting to Eric were G. E. (George) Smith (co-inventor of CCD's), P. J. (Phil) Boddy, and R. E. (Richard) Wagner. I reported to Phil Boddy, along with nine other supervisors.

P. J. (Phil) Boddy

Fifty-seven technical people reported to these ten supervisors. Most aspects of IGFET development and implementation were covered with an impressive array of physicists, electrical engineers, chemists, and software people.

My personal work-place world had once more dramatically changed. Al MacRae was transferred to Holmdel to direct spacecraft and satellite activities. Earlier, Lepselter had gone to Allentown to be Director there. Sam Broydo remained in Murray Hill, and I thought that he would soon be drafted to work in Allentown, and neither the Old Allentown Alliance of Questionable Individuals nor I wanted me to return to work there. The future was unclear.

I do not recall what happened to the crash pad. I think that I retained it for a while. My group was still responsible for diagnostics, and I had Sam Broydo, Mike Grieco, J. A. Heilig, and R. A. (Dick) Kushner, W. S. Lindenberger, V. T. Murphy, W. J. Polito, and W. D. Powell reporting to me. It was still our role to examine devices processed by the BPL, find any repeating faults, and suggest process changes to fix the observed problems. Rusty automatically rejected most suggestions, and we would have to escalate the matter to Phil for resolution.

We soon realized that Phil would resolve conflicts sequentially, allowing each supervisor an equal number of wins. We quickly learned to time our challenges so that Rusty could win things we really did not think mattered, and to save important challenges for our time to win. It was like running a switch controlling the magnet on the roulette wheel. It was a pathetic way to work, but as Sam and I expected, we soon ruled our little roost, and the other supervisors did not seem to understand our strategy.

In early March, Phil Boddy had made a trip to Teletype Corporation, in Skokie IL. I learned that Teletype was a wholly owned subsidiary of Western Electric, and thus a part of AT&T, but with no real connection with Bell Labs. Earlier in the year, Phil had received a call from Frank Alterio, a Teletype Supervisor. Alterio had told Phil that Teletype was pursuing Large Scale Integration (LSI) circuit designs using a p-channel aluminum gate technology. They were interested in finding if any of Phase 2 work might be applicable to their problems. Perhaps because of this call or because of prodding from management, Phil visited Teletype. After his visit, Phil issued a memorandum and reported, "They (Teletype) got into the business in the late 60's because they were looking for LSI at a time when our commitment was low and they got a poor response from Western Electric Company (WECO)-Al (and BTL) as to their needs". Phil concluded, "I think that there is little we can learn from them, although they may have useful experience in aluminum". Phil gave no indication in his report that Teletype was either asking for or needing assistance to improve yields.

Phil sent me a copy of his memorandum, but I took no immediate action. I was concentrating on solving our own problems. I was little interested in either faraway Skokie, Illinois, or Teletype. One day a coworker told me that they had also spoken to Frank Alterio, a Teletype Supervisor, and that there was some indication that Teletype might be interested in tungsten gate technology, including some of our chips. This got my attention. I was feeling pretty fluffed up about our process capabilities, and I called Frank Alterio on the Cornet network, a facility-to-facility non-toll phone trunk system. I introduced myself, and in the course of the conversation I asked, "Would you like to obtain some of our 1 kbit memory chips?" I was confident that he would be properly impressed!

Frank answered, "**No, we are not set up to test such chips. Would you like to have some of the 2 kbit chips that we have made?**" **I was stunned**! These guys in the hinterlands were saying that they were making chips with twice the complexity that we were! Alterio indicated that they were having some yield problems in production, and that he had been asked by his management to review our work. I think that another Teletype team soon visited us, but I have no memory of the visit. If they visited at all, Rusty Buckley, now once again king of his lair, would have hosted them.

Somewhere along the line, the Teletype production problem grew in visibility throughout the rest of the Bell System, as Teletype product shipments to customers slowed to a trickle, and Bell System commitments were not being met. I was told that a three-man high-level team had been dispatched from Western Electric Allentown (WECO-Al) to Teletype to analyze the problem, and to propose possible solutions. I heard little about either the tour or the results, but understood that their primary recommendation to Teletype management was to **"Find a second source!"** I was also led to believe that (Western Electric) Allentown itself had declined to offer either manufacturing or technical assistance. It was my strong impression that Allentown was fighting their own breed of alligators and had nothing left to offer their corporate cousins. Phase 1 might have been declared a success, but Allentown people were still sweating bullets. I don't think the Allentown production lines were shipping enough devices to meet their own demands. Besides having their own production problems, some of their management were still a bit pigheaded and had little sympathy for the Skokie upstarts. Unfortunately for Teletype, it was to turn out that **no one** in the country had the ability to deliver devices with the properties needed for Teletype LSI. **NO ONE!**

The Stinking Ship – Imus Brightens my Mornings

As the days progressed, I became increasingly restive, and could not see that there was a future for me at Bell Labs. It was no longer a question of proving myself. I had proven, at least to my own satisfaction, that I was in at least the same league as the Bell Boys, but I was not happy with the game. The constant "bow and curtsey" routine with Phil was wearing on me. I felt like I was chained in a cage, and the chains were chafing more and more as each week passed. Not only was I growing increasingly weary with my upper management (no surprise here); the daily commute was wearing me down. With the Murray Hill crises put to rest, I did not need the commuting time to organize my thoughts, and the left side of my brain had no great problems to work out. Only the details of the status quo remained. Instead of problem solving while commuting, I began to listen to a really funny morning radio program, "**Imus In The Morning**". My productivity doubtlessly plummeted, but no one was in the office to care.

The Don Imus show was broadcast from WNBC, and the reception was excellent for the whole journey between Allentown and Murray Hill Imus was a highly irreverent personality who spoofed and ridiculed many aspects of our society. He was particularly good when playing "Billy Sol Hargus", an evangelical protestant preacher who sounded much like the guys I had heard late at night on clear channel radio when I lived in Rockville Missouri many years before. The program also had voice imitators who were expert in mimicking political leaders and other popular personalities. Both subjects were very entertaining, but while listening to his show, it was impossible to concentrate on problems. When I finally transferred to Chicago, listening to Imus was one of my greatest losses.

The Imus comic relief was really welcome, but did little to solve the management gridlock at Murray Hill. I had crashed and burned twice before[17], and I was not anxious to repeat the situation for a third time. I decided that I would soon have to make one of three choices - move, quit, or transfer.

One, I could actually move to Murray Hill, but the high housing cost there would dramatically lower my standard of living. The Murray Hill area was very high cost due to the close proximity to New York City, and I would lose a lot of purchasing power if I were to live there. Moreover, such a move would only relieve the long commute. The task would not materially change, and I would still have the same questionable management. I was tired of running on the Murray Hill treadmill. I considered this treadmill a nitwit express. I wanted to avoid becoming a corporate gerbil.

Two, I could quit the Bell System, and look for a job in a commercial enterprise. I was confident of my capabilities, and had no desire to work for a second-rate outfit. I decided that Intel was the only outside company that I would even

---

[17] Once in my senior Year at MU, and once when I told my Director he was hopeless.

consider working for. These guys were one of the best in the business at the time. I had finally succeeded at Bell but could I likewise succeed at Intel? I thought that I probably could. At least it was worth thinking about.

Third, I could possibly go to work for Teletype. Teletype was a wholly owned subsidiary of Western Electric, and thus my years invested in Bell Labs would transfer to Teletype intact. Another benefit of this approach was the fact that my sister lived in a suburb of Chicago, and my brother lived in Madison Wisconsin, a short distance away. We would also be within much easier driving range to both Judy's and my parents, cutting the distance by between one half and two thirds. If I were to take this tack, the nature of my work would change, and almost more importantly, there would be an entirely different management philosophy. A lot would depend upon the nature of the work that I might be involved in if I were I to join Teletype. For sure, this possibility was worth investigating.

In 1973, the spring Electrochemical Society Meeting was held in Chicago. Phil, I, and a number of others decided to attend. With Phil's approval, I also arranged a visit to Teletype during the ECS meeting. Separately from the Chicago trip, I would also soon arrange to take a couple of vacation days to interview at Intel.

A number of BTL people including Phil Boddy and I attended the ECS meeting in Chicago, held in the Blackstone Hotel. As usual, we found a few of the sessions that were interesting, and I actually attended them. I felt only slightly guilty, but try as I would, I had little interest in the meeting proper. I wanted to visit Teletype to help me make a career decision. An event occurred which improved my view of Chicago, and perhaps helped me make my final decision. I discovered Chicago-Style Pizza!

After the first lunch break, Phil returned to the hotel with bright eyes, full belly, and said, "You guys will have to come to lunch with me tomorrow. I have just eaten the most delicious, most unbelievable pizza I have ever tasted!" The next day we complied, along with perhaps a dozen other guys. We all followed him to GENO's in downtown Chicago. After waiting a while in line, we were seated and ordered as Phil suggested. He had understated the case. The crust had a delicate texture and the pizza was loaded with fragrance and exquisite flavor. The crust simply melted away in your mouth. I had never tasted such stuff! On the third day, perhaps seventy-five fellow souls joined the troop. All agreed that this was unlike anything they had ever eaten or heard about. We had been initiated to Chicago-style, world-class, deep-dish pizza! Of more importance, while at the ECS meeting, I made a prearranged visit to Teletype.

The Teletype Visit, Then Intel - 1973

When I visited Teletype, Frank Alterio met me at the R&D guard shack and took me inside. We walked up a half-flight of stairs into the three-story R&D building and immediately into the R&D front offices. Frank introduced me to R. Nordin, Director, and Chuck Winston, Vice President of Teletype R&D. R. Oliver, R. Heeren, Dave Willmott, and possibly others soon joined us.

Chuck explained that Teletype was using LSI chips to replace whole boards, and the entire future of the 12,000 or so Teletype employees in Skokie and their Littlerock plant depended in a fundamental way upon the successful implementation of this approach. By replacing the circuit boards with LSI chips, he intended to offset high in-house manufacturing costs to launch a new wave of terminal devices, the Model 40 line. The boards that were being replaced cost hundreds of dollars to make, and such printers used many boards. The LSI chips That Teletype had designed would tear the competition apart if they could become available on time and in quantity. **No one else in industry was capable of making such devices**, including their main competitor, Digital Equipment Corporation (DEC). Winston was certain that

279

Teletype could meet the challenge. He had staked the company and his career betting upon success!

Winston explained that competitors were suing Teletype and Western Electric for alleged illegal practices. The competition was charging that the Bell Labs was unfairly supporting Teletype, otherwise, "How could the model 40 products possibly be offered at such low anti-competitive prices"? Winston noted that Teletype was not regulated, as was the rest of AT&T. In essence, the competition was charging that the regulated monopoly was unfairly subsidizing Teletype in order to drive other terminal manufactures out of business. Nothing could have been further from the truth, but no one outside could have possibly known that simple fact. The management of the other terminal equipment vendors simply had no one of Winston's vision and capabilities.

Winston had very early on recognized the potential value of LSI chip designs to the Teletype product line. Initially, Teletype had contacted various semiconductor vendors in the industry to design and build custom chips. General Instrument and a fledgling company called Intel were commissioned to design and build some custom devices. These early attempts to acquire custom chips from the industry-at-large failed. Worse yet, parent company Western Electric was committed to chips with such limited complexity[18] that they were of little economic value to Teletype, even if they had been willing to serve as a chip supplier to Teletype. In desperation, Winston had started an internal effort to design and if necessary, build the required chips. He set about acquisition of the equipment to make early models, first in an R&D mode, and finally in production. It was a case of "**succeed or die**"! He also set out to train a cadre of qualified people. He hired the services of the University of Illinois to train the needed Teletype semiconductor crew.

Teletype had designed a number of early chips for the Model 40 family, and the initial device runs in the R&D shop had experienced very good results, a result of some very talented employees. They had done their pricing based on early process results. Based on those early results they had committed to production, and were ramping up the product line. However, they were having trouble achieving adequate yields in the factory. The devices that were causing the most trouble were the magnet driver chips. These chips operated at 25 volts and high currents, a bad combination for the technology they had implemented. These chips were experiencing very low production yields. The low yields were

---

[18] Jack Morton had done his best to keep "the right scale of integration" a Bell System mantra.

limiting shipments of the Model 40 line-at-a-time printer, a flagship product of the new product line. He felt certain that the yield problem could be overcome. Chuck was both a consistent realist and yet a determined optimist. He was a man to admire.

After introductions, donuts and discussion, I was given a tour of the facilities. Alterio's group was located on the second floor, with several laser labs adjacent next door. I was introduced to his people, but there was little time for discussion with them. A small **R&D facility** about double the size of crash pad was located on the first floor. Another pair of enclosed rooms, called the **EPI labs,** was located in nearby factory space in a building identified as T3. About a half block west of the EPI lab, we toured the production facility, also located in building T3.

The Teletype people looked a little strange to me. Manners and demeanor seemed a little coarser than that at Bell, and the educational level was clearly not as high. On the other hand, it was evident that these people did not know that what they were trying to do was impossible. They were just trying to do it. These guys had not bought BTL's Jack Morton small-chip mantra. At the time Teletype was starting its IC effort, Morton had decreed that the right chip size was around 0.04 in by 0.04 in. Teletype's first chip design needed a die size of 0.202 in by 0.201 in. and it took them several months of hard design work to make it that small. **They also could not find a commercial mask shop to make acceptable masks of such sizes.** Bell similarly could not help. They had not yet developed the need to make such large area masks, except perhaps for the Phase 2 device, a one-of-a-kind effort.

Teletype had set up their own metallization system to coat glass blanks with tantalum metal. They obtained a YAG laser from Bell Labs, fitted a commercial x-y milling machine table with interferometers, and built their own control computer to coordinate laser shots with table position to convert the metallized blanks into master reticules. The mask engine was driven by output from the commercial Applicon[19] computer-aided design system that was used for actual circuit layouts. They also bought a step-and-repeat camera from an American Company, and bought two of the best lenses they could find from Zeiss. They bought 10x and 4x reduction lenses, the best that they could buy. This system had been used to make most of the mask sets up to that date. These guys would not take no for an answer!

At the end of the day, I thanked them all for sharing their accomplishments with me, and went on my way to

---

[19] Teletype had been a key partner with Applicon in the development of Applicon's chip design package.

ponder the situation. I was impressed with their efforts, but was not yet convinced that this would be a new home for my work.

I had made contact with Intel and they arranged airfare, transportation, and a hotel in Santa Clara. As I flew over the Midwest and then over the Rocky Mountains listening to the Moody Blues, I wondered if I could ever find a peaceful place to work, or whether the lack of peace was inherent in me. I fell asleep without resolving the matter, and awakened as we neared San Hose. When I visited Intel, I was properly impressed with the work that they allowed me to see. They were indeed masters of semiconductor technology. They stressed that the only projects they worked on were initiated from the top (Whoops!). The upper management people at Intel were true leaders in the field. They were owners, managers, and true innovators as well. It became obvious to me that if I were to work at Intel, work would essentially be a series of replays of Phase 2, "I want THIS, make it work, NOW!" I thought long and hard about the proposition. Success here could result in advancement, riches, and prestige, unlike the relatively meaningless exercise at Bell. Failure was not considered a possibility to guard against.

On the return trip, I stopped to see Mom and Dad in Missouri, and discussed the situation with them. I told them about my alternatives. I had narrowed things down to either taking the job at Teletype in Chicago, or with Intel on the west coast. They said only what I already knew. "If your career depends upon it, go to the west coast. Otherwise, we surely would like to have you and your family closer to us in Chicago".

I had not realized just how much I wanted to be nearer to my family, even though the move would separate me from my eastern friends, and end an important chapter in my life. I had achieved at least some success at Bell Labs, but felt the need to move on. Whether it was changes in me, changes in BTL management, or in the larger semiconductor industry that made me want to leave, I could not say. All I knew was that I felt compelled to try my wings in a new venue. Perhaps in the new surroundings, I would again find fertile ground, somewhat as I had upon return to Murray Hill, from Allentown.

As usual, the visit with my folks helped to calm my mind a bit, and I returned to Allentown a little less conflicted.

Mom and Dad at Buddy's - 1973

Buddy's Family in Madison Wisconsin - 1973
Katherine, Carol, Buddy, Chris, and Wade

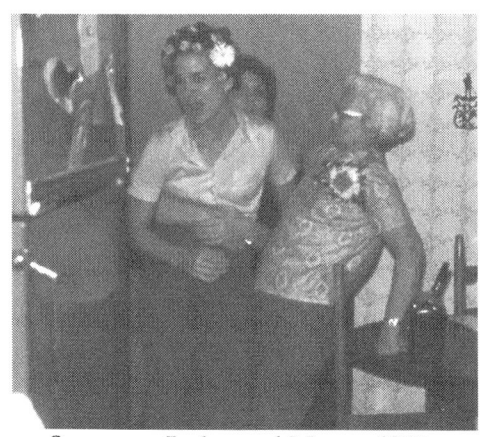

Suzanne, Judy, and Mom - 1974

The prospect of being once more far away from our families would help us to decide against moving to the west coast. We settled upon returning to the Midwest.

Teletype It Is!

Back in Allentown, both Judy and I were in favor of being near family, and decided that we would not take this particular opportunity to return to California. We decided to go to Illinois instead. Not only would I get out of Murray Hill, I could readily transfer to Teletype. My service date would bridge, and all benefits would remain intact. As a transferee, I was eligible for all their assistance in guaranteeing a sale price on the Allentown home, moving costs, and company assistance in buying a place in my new location.

As I have said before, Sam Broydo and I had become very good friends as well as good coworkers. One of the hardest parts of going to Chicago was the need to leave the company of such a remarkable man. Here was a guy born and raised a half-planet away, under a different social system, with a different religious background, and yet we had forged such a friendship! It would have been great if the two of us could continue to work together, but at the time, Sam had much more to do for the Bell Semiconductor effort, so it was not even a possibility that he would leave the nest. A number of years later, we would almost work together again, this time at PARC at Xerox in Palo Alto, but that is another story that I will get to in my next book.

    I told Phil about my decision to leave and I think that he well understood. We set a final date of 13 September 1973. Sam Broydo organized the going away party. The going-away party began at noon. I was driven to the party so that I would not have to worry about getting back to work. Marty Lepselter, Al Mac Rae, Sam Broydo, David Thomas, Geoffrey Garrett, Fabian Pease, George Smith, Phil Boddy, Harry Boll, Don Scharfetter, Dawan Kahng, Bob Kerwin, Joe Ligenza, Dick Kushner, John Dalton, Mike Tomsky, Pete Byrnes, Bill Craft, and a host of others gave me a rousing and somewhat alcoholic sendoff. We all ate, joked, drank, and talked until around three in the afternoon. There were a few short speeches and presentations. Al MacRae gave me the 8 1/2 x 11 framed montage shown below:

I recall most of the deep inner meanings of the sacred symbols: The toy truck labeled "Mattel" refers to my strongly stated desire to make something meaningful in the Buckley line, not just test chips. I had told Garret and Thomas, "If I wanted to make toys, I'd have gone to work for Mattel"! The matchbook cover refers to the place often used as Al's and my conference area, Auntie Mame's (eating and drinking establishment), in Stirling New Jersey. The sandbox refers to the part of our workplace that I enjoyed the most, the "Crash Pad". The cat in the corner refers to **"The Cat Pee Syndrome"**, named for my tomcat, Fu Manchu, whereby people are inclined to make a mark on their work, even if it is wholly inappropriate. The yoyo represents all the people who didn't have a clue as to what was going on. The two talking boxes refer to my occasional references to the fact that BTL people liked to live safely within their (fortress) cubicles, and did not like to work in teams. The center artifact represents **"metal falling off the phase 2 devices"**, as I have described in the text. The composite picture in the lower left part of the picture is a clear message to me regarding proper behavior in the corporate world. The message is: **_"Wear a white shirt and be a sneak._ In other words, if your boss wants you to wear a white shirt, do so to satisfy him, but then do your thing with the freedom that you have obtained by sucking up to your boss".** The picture gave all a good laugh, and in the future, I attempted to follow Al's excellent advice, with some limited success.

Many of my friends and coworkers were there to wish me well, many of them wondering, "How the hell can **I** get out of this trap?" Some others were doubtless thinking, "Thank goodness he's gone!" Others were merely enjoying a good party. Fortunately, there were volunteer designated drivers.

Party Guys:
L ro R: (?), Earnie Lebate, (?), Goeffry Garret,
Marty Lepselter, Al MacRae, three others, & Dick Kushner

Party Talk, L to R:
Herb Waggener, Al MacRae, Goeffry Garret, & George Smith

291

People slowly began leaving, and not surprisingly, some were in worse shape than others. I was returned to the rear entrance of building 2, along with several other celebrants, including Mike Tomsky and Phil Boddy. As Mike got to the sidewalk, he did a simple swoon, and faded gently to the sidewalk, a little impaired. Phil apparently did not notice, and tripped over him a bit, but kept on walking as he went on into the Lab. As more people arrived back at work, Mike was picked up, escorted to the coffee machine, and given a lot of fresh air. Time would heal Mike's minor bruises and lift the fog. As I made my last round of the day to say goodbye, I walked into Phil's office for a final handshake. Phil quickly arose from his chair and accidentally swept his desk clean with his forearm. He did not seem to mind, and wished me well. I too wished him well and left him to pick up the mess on the floor and otherwise.

For me, the day was traumatic. In some real sense, I had succeeded at Bell Labs, but it was an empty victory. I felt compelled to leave my friends, and was certain that I would miss them. I was equally certain that I would not miss Bell Labs upper management. A new opportunity with new challenges lay ahead! I could not know that the road ahead would be so rocky and finally sputter to an inglorious end, choreographed or at least assisted by my old compatriots at

Allentown. Eventually, even the stalwarts at Allentown would also be forced to walk the plank, but that process would take many years.

The Transfer Process Begins!

Judy and I had some getting ready to do. We put our house at 713 S. Ott St. up for sale. We were transferring within the Bell System, so we were eligible for assistance in relocation, just as we had been when we were transferred from Murray Hill to Allentown in 1966, and when were transferred back to Murray Hill in 1969. This time we owned a house, not a foundation, so there were no real complications, just an interruption of our normal activities.

The company transfer policy covered a number of items. First, Teletype agreed to purchase our old house at a predetermined market price if we were unable to sell it. Second, the company would reimburse moving costs, and at least partially offset any difference in housing costs incurred as a result of the transfer. Third, I was allowed five months of transportation and temporary living costs prior to moving into a new home. In short, Teletype took care of us!

My last day of work at Murray Hill was 13 September 1973. As part of the checkout procedure, I had to walk over to the same personnel office in Building 3 where I had arrived on 31 July 1961, almost twelve years before. The individuals were different, but the place looked the same. They asked, "Why are you leaving?" and I replied, "To have a better tomorrow!" "Oh, OK." They said. I signed papers agreeing to whatever, I know not what, and my trusty badge was replaced with a paper pass good only for that day.

On the next Monday morning, I flew to Chicago for my first day at my new job. It would be some time before Judy, Mark, John, and Shawn would become residents of Illinois. First, a suitable home for our family would have to be found, and second, I considered it essential to immediately begin work on the various ills afflicting the Teletype semiconductor effort. Without a solution to these problems in the pretty near future, there would soon be some 12,000 Teletype employees, including me, looking for jobs in Skokie Illinois, Little Rock Arkansas, and various other places!

Thus ended what I hoped would be my last employment at Bell Labs. It wasn't. I would briefly return once more in 1986, while (the now old) OLDAT&T[20] was in the process of deleting Teletype. I would again rejoin Lepselter while the Teletype R & D building was razed to the ground, the basements filled, at least figuratively sprinkled with salt, and covered with asphalt to complete the parking

---

[20] The current AT&T Company is only related in name to the AT&T of the 1960s through 89.

area, and the balance of the Teletype facility turned into a Skokie Shopping Mall.

Postscript

In 1973, I transferred from Bell Labs to the Teletype Corporation, Skokie Illinois, as a supervisor in the semiconductor processing area. The Teletype Semiconductor effort was in deep doo-doo when I arrived. While at Teletype, we organized a multi-man-year rescue operation and broke a production logjam, thus allowing a lot of Teletype product to ship, resulting in some level of corporate prosperity. In the late seventies, a general economic downturn caused layoffs, but our internal continuity of effort remained. After a lot of pain, I was eventually promoted to Project Director, and led a superb Semiconductor Technology Development Group, building and staffing a technologist's dream I named the Ultra Large Scale Integration facility, or **ULSI** for short. While I was working at Teletype, in May 1980, my first wife, Judith, divorced me. After drinking a whole lot of scotch whiskey, I eventually recovered, and again prospered. To my dismay and disappointment, OLDAT&T[21] eventually shut down the Teletype Company altogether. The 1973 to 1985 era is described in the book, titled, "**Teletype, We Made That Data**

---

[21] The term "OLDAT&T" is used to distinguish the old company from the AT&T of the 2000s.

Move!" - subtitle – **"The Development of Teletype Custom Logic Technology that ended along with The Demise of the Teletype Corporation"** currently in final editing. In 1985, I left Teletype in disgust/despair and quit semiconductor process development forever.

I returned to New Jersey and briefly worked for Bell Labs while waiting to join Martin Lepselter in a new startup initially proposed by the AT&T venture group. In 1986, I joined the start-up company Lepton Inc., founded by him. Marty formed Lepton to extend and commercialize the EBES4 electron beam exposure technology previously developed by Bell Labs.

I was eventually lucky enough to be accepted by a marvelous lady I had met in Skokie, Darlene E. (Evenson) Knutson, and we were married on 7 February 1987 in Oldwick, New Jersey. While at Lepton, I initially worked on process technology needed to test the EBES4 machine being developed, and eventually assumed responsibility for the development of various essential precision mechanical components. When I left Lepton in 1994, my title was "Executive Director of Technology Development".

After leaving Lepton, I became an independent consultant. Coworker/partner Kazimirez Przydzial and I co-invented a medical device sterilization technique. We received a patent, "Method and Apparatus for Sterilizing Medical Devices Using Glow Discharges", # 5,573,732, which we eventually abandoned.

I briefly signed on with Medjet Inc. a company founded by Eugene Gordon, and was soon appointed Vice President in Charge of Technology. In 1995, I resigned from Medjet Inc. to move to Wisconsin in order to pursue the continued development of quality-of-life products and technology.

The work at Bell Labs, Lepton, Medjet, and with Kazimirez Przydzial, 1985 to 1995, will be described in the book tentatively titled, **"Electron Beams, Water Jets, and Medical Devices"-** subtitle – **"Making the EBES4 for Photomasks, Shaping Corneas with Water Jets, and Making Ozone".**

After moving to Wisconsin, I worked on several medical devices and in 1999, patented a prosthetic hip joint, 5,879,407, "Wear Resistant Ball and Socket Joint" that I expected to have extremely low internal wear characteristics, and thus require fewer repair or revision surgeries.

In 2004, I momentarily paused my technical pursuits to document my path through what has been a mixture of exciting, disappointing, and satisfying times.

In 2006, Darlene and I sold the hip joint patent rights to Biomet Manufacturing Corp., a major Orthopaedic Company. Following a period of accommodation to our new situation, I was able to again return to my *quality of life* mission. The book describing this his era, 1995 to 2007 or thereabouts, is currently named, **"From Employment to Independent"** - subtitle - **"Not Dropping Out, Just Advancing in a Different Direction"**!

In late 2007, I temporarily set aside continuing work on my memoirs to concentrate on another project that I call "***Sky Shield***", involving certain aspects of global warming. I have continued to work on this project through early 2010.

A patent relative to this material has been applied for, and technical refinement continues. Only time will tell in what way, if any, this attempt to make a major quality-of-life impact for citizens of our planet will work out. In the meantime, I am using some of my time to continue writing my memoirs, and am also working on other, smaller projects. Thus, I continue to work.

United States Patent [19]
Waggener

[11] Patent Number: 5,879,407
[45] Date of Patent: Mar. 9, 1999

[54] **WEAR RESISTANT BALL AND SOCKET JOINT**

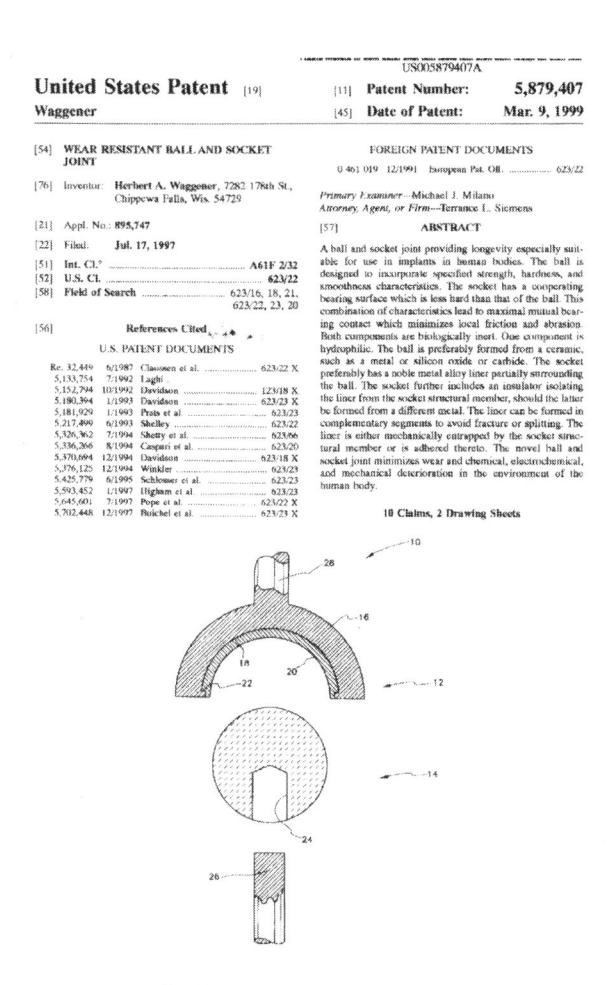

[76] Inventor: Herbert A. Waggener, 7282 178th St., Chippewa Falls, Wis. 54729

[21] Appl. No.: 895,747
[22] Filed: Jul. 17, 1997
[51] Int. Cl.⁶ A61F 2/32
[52] U.S. Cl. 623/22
[58] Field of Search 623/16, 18, 21, 623/22, 23, 20

[56] **References Cited**

U.S. PATENT DOCUMENTS

Re. 32,449	6/1987	Claussen et al.	623/22 X
5,133,754	7/1992	Laghi	
5,152,794	10/1992	Davidson	123/18 X
5,190,394	1/1993	Davidson	623/23 X
5,181,929	1/1993	Prats et al.	623/23
5,217,499	6/1993	Shelley	623/22
5,326,362	7/1994	Shetty et al.	623/66
5,336,266	8/1994	Caspari et al.	623/20
5,370,694	12/1994	Davidson	623/18 X
5,376,125	12/1994	Winkler	623/23
5,425,779	6/1995	Schlosser et al.	623/23
5,593,452	1/1997	Higham et al.	623/23
5,645,601	7/1997	Pope et al.	623/22 X
5,702,448	12/1997	Buechel et al.	623/23 X

FOREIGN PATENT DOCUMENTS

0 461 019 12/1991 European Pat. Off. 623/22

Primary Examiner—Michael J. Milano
Attorney, Agent, or Firm—Terrance L. Siemens

[57] **ABSTRACT**

A ball and socket joint providing longevity especially suitable for use in implants in human bodies. The ball is designed to incorporate specified strength, hardness, and smoothness characteristics. The socket has a cooperating bearing surface which is less hard than that of the ball. This combination of characteristics lead to maximal mutual bearing contact which minimizes local friction and abrasion. Both components are biologically inert. One component is hydrophilic. The ball is preferably formed from a ceramic, such as a metal or silicon oxide or carbide. The socket preferably has a noble metal alloy liner partially surrounding the ball. The socket further includes an insulator isolating the liner from the socket structural member, should the latter be formed from a different metal. The liner can be formed in complementary segments to avoid fracture or splitting. The liner is either mechanically entrapped by the socket structural member or is adhered thereto. The novel ball and socket joint minimizes wear and chemical, electrochemical, and mechanical deterioration in the environment of the human body.

10 Claims, 2 Drawing Sheets

A poor copy of Hip Joint Patent #5,879,407 Abstract

Appendix 1 – HAW Patents Held or Co-held as of June 2010

"Process for Preparation of Stabilized Metal Film Resistors", Patent #3,457,148

"Switching Network", Patent #3,504,131

"Etchant for Precision Etching of Semiconductors", Patent #3,506,509

"Method for Producing Passivated PN Junctions by Ion Beam Implantation", Patent #3,615,874

"Method for Producing Passivated PN Junctions by Ion Beam Implantation", Patent #3,617,391

"Electroplating Method", Patent #3,627,648

"Electrochemically Controlled Shaping of Semiconductors", Patent # 3,689,389

"Precision Etching of Semiconductors", Patent # 3,765,969

"Multiple-Level Metallization for Integrated Circuits", Patent # 3,837,907

"Etching Si_3N_4", Patent # 3,715,249

"Field Effect Transistor Structures and Methods", Patent # 3,823,352

"IGFET Memory System", Patent # 3,771,147

"Method of Manufacturing an Insulated Gate Field-effect Transistor Therefore in a Silicon Wafer" Patent # 4,317,276

"Method for Manufacturing an Integrated Circuit Device", Patent # 4,485,553

"Silicon Nozzle Structures and Method of Manufacture" Patent # 4,733,823

"Method for Fabricating X-ray Masks", Patent # 4,932,872

"X-ray Masks, their Fabrication and Use", Patent # 5,020,083

"Method for Producing a Semiconductor Device Using an Electron Beam Exposure Tool and Apparatus for Producing the Device", Patent # 5,025,165

"Method and Apparatus for Sterilizing Medical Devices Using Glow Discharges", Patent # 5,573,732

"Stabilizing Support Mechanism for Electron Beam Apparatus", Patent # 5,644,137

"Wear Resistant Ball and Socket Joint" Patent # 5,879,407

I expect that there are more to come. - haw

In June 2010, I finally sold my last Corvair, a red 1965 Monza convertible, and my accumulated horde of Corvair parts, thereby ending a love affair of over 49 years. It was time to move on to more important matters.

Made in the USA
Columbia, SC
06 November 2023